Kids Weaving

Sarah Swett

Photographs by Chris Hartlove

Illustrations by Lena Corwin

STC CRAFT | A MELANIE FALICK BOOK   NEW YORK

For my grandmothers, Catherine Carton Swett and Randall Williams Chanler,
who showed me that there is nothing more pleasurable than making things by hand,
and nothing more beautiful than things that that are handmade.

Published in 2005 by
STC Craft | A Melanie Falick Book
115 West 18th Street
New York, NY 10011
www.abramsbooks.com

Library of Congress Cataloging-in-Publication Data

Swett, Sarah.
  Kids weaving / Sarah Swett ; photographs by Chris Hartlove ;
illustrations by Lena Corwin.
    p. cm.
  Includes index.
  ISBN 1-58479-467-4
1. Hand weaving--Juvenile literature. I. Title.

TT848.S96 2005
746.1'4--dc22
2005000650

The text of this book was composed in Sauna designed by Underware

Printed in Thailand
10 9 8 7 6 5 4 3 2 1
FIRST PRINTING

Edited by Melanie Falick
Designed by Jessi Rymill (based on a design by Jennifer Wagner)
Production by Alexis Mentor

Stewart, Tabori & Chang is a subsidiary of

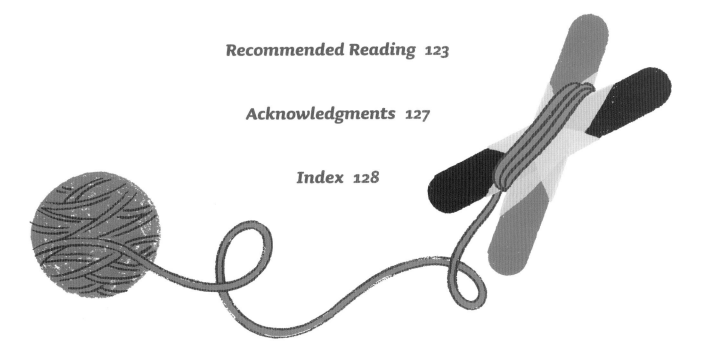

Introduction

Weaving is the process of interlacing strips of paper, strands of yarn, and even sticks to make new things that are wonderful to look at, touch, wear, and use. Weaving is everywhere, but we see it so often that sometimes we don't even recognize it! If you have ever pulled on a pair of blue jeans, tied a bandanna, or snuggled into a jacket, it is likely that you have worn clothes made from woven cloth. It is also possible that the rug on your floor, the sheets on your bed, and even your blanket are woven.

For longer than most of us can imagine, people have been connecting sticks and threads to make things that they have needed to survive—fences, clothing, and baskets. No one really knows how long ago people started to weave, but we do know that the basic technique has not changed in five thousand years. Pictures on the walls of the Pyramids in Egypt show people weaving. When Christopher Columbus sailed from Spain to the New World, he was propelled by sails made of woven cloth. Most cloth today is made by machines, but there have been times when people spent more time making cloth by hand than preparing food.

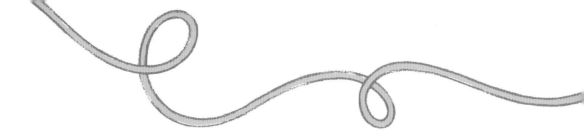

In **Kids Weaving** you will learn techniques that you can use to make everything from paper note cards and willow fences to bags, scarves, and even rugs. You can weave projects for yourself or to give away as gifts. You can weave with your friends, by yourself, or while listening to music. Learning to weave is a bit like learning to ride a bike or play an instrument: the more you practice the easier it becomes. Because the projects in this book are arranged in order of increasing skill, it's a good idea to try a few projects in Chapters 1 and 2 before starting projects in Chapters 3 or 4.

Kids Weaving is the beginning of an exciting journey. When you weave, you are connecting yourself with people and places around the world and through time. As you interlace your threads and sticks and pieces of paper you are connecting your own history and your own work with the history of all people, learning skills that are as old as time to make things that you can use today.

weaving
without a loom

When people think about weaving,
they often think about something that happens on a
frame called a loom. But, you can actually weave without a loom,
using only your hands and simple materials you are likely to find
around the house. The techniques are fun and easy and a great way
to begin to understand how weaving works: by interlacing up-and-down
materials (like yarn or paper) with side-to-side materials, you make
a whole new thing that is a combination of both the up and down
and the back and forth parts.

In this chapter, we will explore three of these "no loom" kinds of weaving:
Woven Note Cards and Dancing Map Dolls made with paper;
a Fairy Fence created with sticks and moss;
and a Friendship Bracelet made with yarn.

Easy Going!
Charlie learns the basics
of weaving the easy way—
by making a chain of
Dancing Map Dolls.

warp & weft

THERE ARE TWO PARTS TO EVERY WEAVING, ONE PART THAT GOES UP AND DOWN AND ANOTHER PART THAT GOES SIDE TO SIDE. THE UP AND DOWN PART IS CALLED THE WARP. THE SIDE TO SIDE PART IS CALLED THE WEFT.

The warp and the weft are usually made of strands of something such as yarn, paper, or sticks. Weaving is the process of connecting or interlacing the up and down strands, the warp, with the side to side strands, the weft, to make a new thing, such as a piece of cloth.

When you start to weave, the first thing that you do is prepare the up and down strands, the warp. This usually means doing some measuring, cutting, or winding, depending on the type of weaving that you are doing.

The second thing you do is bring the strand of weft from one side to the other—left to right or right to left. The weft goes over and under, over and under the warp.

In this book we will use a lot of different materials to practice this and to create great projects, but all of them involve exactly the same two parts—the up and down part, the warp, that you set up first, and the side to side part, the weft, that you weave over and under the warp.

By changing the materials and the setup techniques and the way that you bring the weft over and under the warp, you can make all of the projects in this book and a million other things as well.

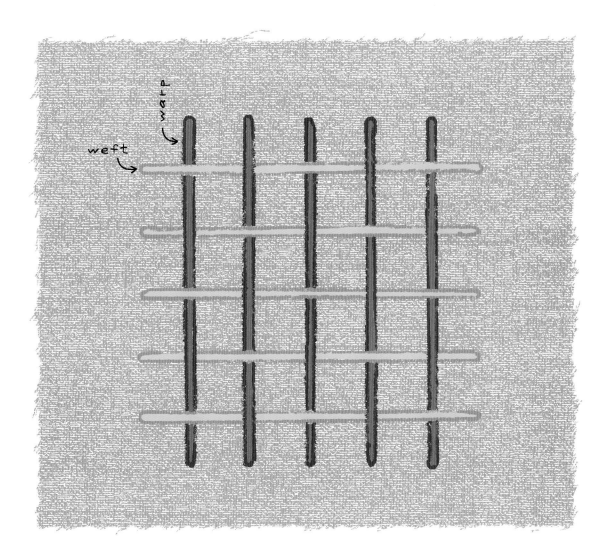

Since they both start with the letter W, remembering which part of a weaving is the warp and which part is the weft can be confusing. One way to remind yourself is to think that the word "weft" rhymes with "left." "Left to right" and "right to left" are the same as "side to side."

checkerboard
note cards

PAPER IS A FUN AND EASY MATERIAL WITH which to learn the basic steps of weaving. In this project you combine 2 pieces of colored paper or cardstock to make a new design. First you make cuts in a folded piece of paper or cardstock to make strands for the warp, the up and down part. Then you cut another piece of paper or cardstock into strips that you weave from side to side for the weft. What you end up with is an entirely new design with colors that appear and disappear where the warp and the weft overlap each other.

materials

- 1 ($5\frac{1}{2}$" × $8\frac{1}{2}$") PIECE CONSTRUCTION PAPER OR CARDSTOCK (*available at craft and art supply stores*)

- 1 (4" × $5\frac{1}{2}$") PIECE CONSTRUCTION PAPER OR CARDSTOCK IN A DIFFERENT COLOR

- PENCIL

- SCISSORS

- TRANSPARENT TAPE

1   prepare warp

Your larger piece of paper will be the warp, the up and down part that you prepare first. Place it on a table and fold it in half so that the fold is at the top and the top and bottom of the card each measure $5\frac{1}{2}$" wide. The fold will be the top of your warp. You will be weaving only on the front of the folded paper.

Starting at the bottom of the front and about $\frac{1}{2}$" from one side, cut to the fold as shown in the illustration on page 12.

Make more cuts, each about $\frac{1}{2}$" apart, across the front of the folded paper. The front of the paper is now floppy and looks like a string skirt. This is your warp, the up and down part.

Colorful Greetings
Use your favorite colors
of paper to make your
very own notecards.

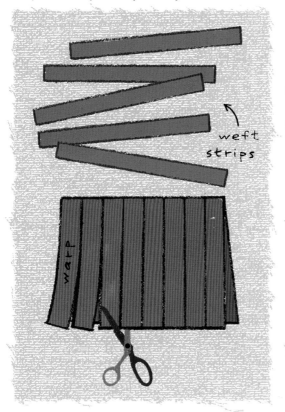

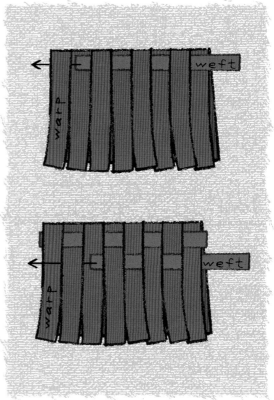

2   prepare weft

The smaller piece of colored paper will be your weft, the side-to-side part.

Starting at the 4" edge, cut the colored paper into strips about $\frac{1}{4}$" – $\frac{1}{2}$" wide and $5\frac{1}{2}$" long. Cut them all the way through to make separate strips.

3   start weaving

Pick up one of the loose strips of colored paper (the weft strips).

Starting from one side of the folded paper (the warp), bring the strip of colored paper over the first of the up-and-down warp strips, then under the second, over the

Continue like this—weave one weft strip over, under, over, under and the next strip under, over, under, over—until the entire front of the card is woven and looks like a checkerboard. Each time you start a new row, take a look at what you did on the row before and make sure to do the opposite.

4 *finishing*

Put a piece of tape along each edge of the back of the weaving to keep the strips from coming unwoven.

Step 4 *Tape woven edges on back of weaving*

back of weaving

third, then under the fourth, repeating "over, under, over, under" until you have woven it all the way across to the other side. Gently push the colored paper strip up as close as possible to the fold at the top.

Choose a second weft strip, and weave it under the warp strips you went over last time and over the ones that you went under, until it is all the way across. Gently push the second weft strip up as close as possible to the first weft strip.

Mixed Up!
Weave one or more
colors of weft strips
through a photo warp
to create a mixed-up
memory note card.

Explore and Discover

ONCE YOU'VE MADE ONE NOTE CARD AND UNDERSTAND HOW PAPER IS WOVEN, IT'S EASY TO GET SUPER-CREATIVE. HERE ARE SOME IDEAS TO GET YOU STARTED.

Crazy Cuts

Instead of cutting the warp and weft in straight lines, make cuts curvy or make them with decorative scissors such as pinking shears. Also try cutting up and weaving with weft strips in different colors.

Checkerboard Photograph

Instead of using a folded piece of construction paper for your warp, use a photograph (with a parent's permission). When you cut the photo into strips to make the warp, cut almost to the top but not all the way through—leave about $\frac{1}{2}$" uncut photograph at the top to stop the weft strip when you push it up. You might find that the thinner you cut your strips the more the picture shows up, or that you only want to weave certain parts of the photograph so that you can see special parts of it, such as faces.

Wild Photo Combos

Weave together 2 same-size photos. For example, weave pictures of you and your dog, or you and your best friend.

Place Mats

Use an $8\frac{1}{2}$" x 11" piece of paper for the up and down warp and an 8" x 10" photo (or color copy of a photo) for the side to side weft. To protect from spills and drips, seal the place mat between 2 sheets of clear contact paper or have it laminated at a copy shop. Of course, you can also use it just the way that it is. When it gets covered with ice cream drips or spaghetti sauce, put it in the recycling bin and make another.

Black-and-White and Color

Print out a digital photo twice, once in color, once in black and white. Or make a black-and-white copy and a color copy of a regular photo. Weave together and see what happens!

Secret Codes

Write words or messages on pieces of paper that will be the warp and weft. When they are woven together, it will look like a jumble of letters. Send this to a friend who will have to unweave it and reassemble the original pieces of paper to decode the message.

dancing
map dolls

ONE OF THE FUN THINGS ABOUT WEAVING with paper is neither of the parts have to be square; you can cut your warp, the up and down part, and your weft, the side to side part, into any shape that you can imagine. Paper dolls come in many interesting shapes and sizes, but when you make them from maps and decorate them with strips of colored paper, they become even more fascinating.

1 prepare map

Unfold the map lengthwise so that it is long and narrow as shown in the illustration on page 18.

Cut off one segment at the fold, making sure to cut through all of the layers. The number of dolls you can make holding hands at the same time is equal to the number of layers of this segment.

materials

MAP, APPROXIMATELY 4" × 9" LONG WHEN FOLDED SHUT (*available at gas stations, automobile clubs, bookstores, and in the glove compartments of cars— make sure that no one needs the map you are using*)

SEVERAL PIECES 4" × 5" CONSTRUCTION PAPER IN DIFFERENT COLORS (OR USE PAPER FROM OLD CATALOGS AND MAGAZINES)

PENCIL

SCISSORS

TRANSPARENT TAPE

Remember When!
Preserve special memories of your home state or a vacation destination by weaving a map of the area into a line of dancing boys or girls.

Step 1 ***Prepare map***

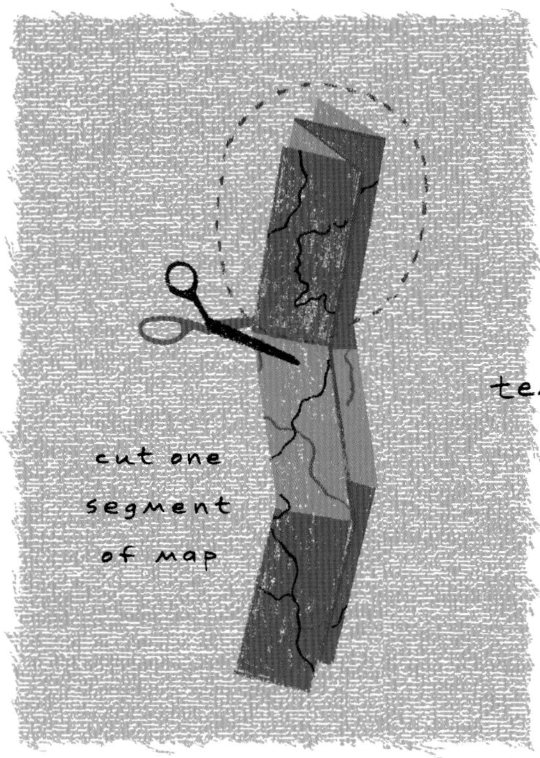

Step 2 ***Trace and cut out doll shape***

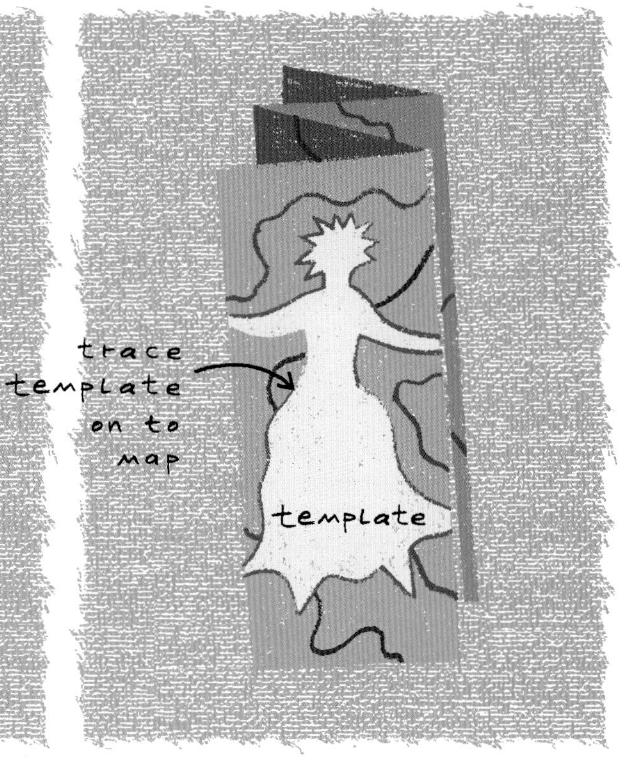

2 *make dolls*

Photocopy and enlarge one of the doll templates (either the boy or girl) on page 124 by 165 percent. The doll should be about 8" tall after it is enlarged. Carefully cut out the shape of the photocopied doll.

Place the cut-out template onto the top of your prepared folded map segment, making sure that the arms go to the edges or even stick off the edges a little bit. Trace the outline of the doll onto the front of the folded map section.

Cutting through all of the layers, cut out around the dolls everywhere EXCEPT where their hands and skirts (for girls) or hands and knees (for boys) meet at the folds. Unfold them and watch your dolls dance hand in hand.

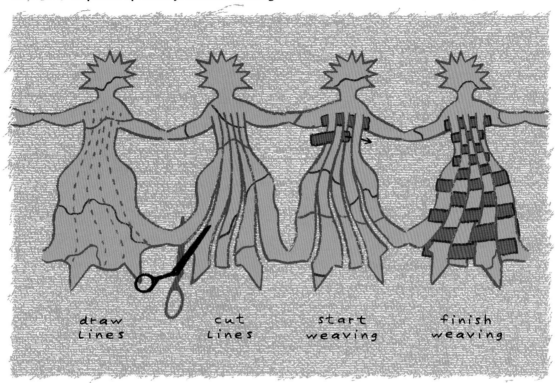

draw
lines

cut
lines

start
weaving

finish
weaving

3 prepare warp and weft

Carefully draw light lines onto the dolls like the dotted lines on the template. Cut along these lines, one doll at a time. The doll is now your warp, the up and down part of the weaving, and it is floppy.

Cut the colored paper into separate strips about 4" long and $\frac{1}{2}$" wide. These strips will be your weft, the part of the weaving that goes from side to side.

4 weave weft strips across warp

Weave a weft strip of colored paper over then under, then over then under the strips of warp—the floppy strips that you cut in the dolls' clothing. Weave it from one side of the doll to the other, leaving the ends sticking out of both sides of the doll. Gently push the weft strip up toward the top of the doll.

Weave another weft strip across. This time weave it under the warp strips that you went over last time, and over the warp strips that you went under. Gently push it up until it is next to the first strip.

Continue to alternate between weft strips that go over then under and weft strips that go under then over, until the warp is completely woven. Remember to notice what you did in the last row so that you know what to do with the next one.

When the figure is completely woven, put some tape on the back of the dolls to hold the strips in place (see how this is done for the note cards on page 13). With your scissors, carefully trim the bits of colored paper sticking out beyond the edge of your doll.

Cut and weave the next doll and this time try something new—use different colors or cut your weft strips wider or narrower, or weave only a skirt or pants.

Line Dancing!
After cutting around the doll shape on the map (except where their hands and skirt or hands and knees meet at the fold), unfold the map to reveal the dolls dancing in a line.

Map Doll Variations

LET EACH OF YOUR MAP DOLLS EXPRESS HIS OR HER UNIQUE PERSONALITY BY TRYING OUT THE VARIATIONS SUGGESTED HERE OR BY COMING UP WITH YOUR OWN VARIATIONS.

Cutting

Instead of straight lines, cut both your warp and your weft into curvy strips.

Color

Use different colored weft strips to weave different pieces of clothing—one color for the top and another for the pants or skirt.

Weaving

For some of the dolls weave only the skirt or pants, leaving the shirts as solid maps.

Notice: Colors change when they are woven as warp and weft. If you put a bright color next to a dark color it can make them both look more intense. If the warp and weft colors are very similar, it can be hard to see the weaving.

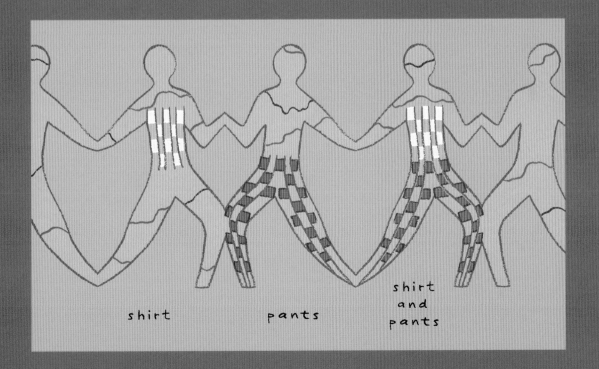

fairy **garden**

WITH THIS PROJECT, YOU WILL LEARN TO
make woven fences and to create your own magical world——a place where you might live if you were a fairy. You can make your fairy garden inside or outside. If you ever need bigger fences, just follow the instructions using bigger sticks. And if you want to use sticks to weave a magical space big enough for you and your friends to hang out in, turn to page 26.

materials

- SHALLOW BOWL OR FLOWER POT—— 8" TO 10" WIDE AT THE TOP AND 2" TO 4" DEEP

- 6 TO 8 CUPS GOOD GARDEN DIRT OR POTTING SOIL

- FOR EACH FENCE: 6 STICKS——EACH ABOUT 6" LONG AND SLIGHTLY THINNER THAN A PENCIL

- HANDFUL OF FINE FLEXIBLE TWIGS, GRASSES, PINE NEEDLES, OR FEATH- ERS, 8" TO 10" LONG

- PRUNING SHEARS OR STRONG UTILITY SCISSORS

- MOSS——ABOUT 10 SMALL PIECES, EACH ABOUT 2" × 2" (*see page 25*), PLUS FERNS OR GRASSES GROWING ALONG- SIDE, IF DESIRED

- SHELLS, STONES, AND OTHER SMALL EMBELLISHMENTS

1 *prepare soil*

Put 2" to 3" soil into your pot. With your fingers, make hills and valleys in the soil.

2 *build fence*

Make a 4"- to 6"-long straight line in the soil where you want a fence to be. Poke the 6 sticks into the dirt along the fence line, about 1" to $1\frac{1}{2}$" apart and as deep as you can. These sticks are your warp, the up and down part of your weaving.

Gently weave a fine, flexible twig or piece of grass in and out of the warp sticks——over, under, over, under, until it is all the way across. Push the ends of the twig down toward the soil.

Finding Fairyland!
Did you ever wonder where fairies live?
If you look closely at mosses it is possible
to imagine a fairy wading through the tiny
upright stems, heading for a magical
little house just out of sight.

Gently weave your second weft twig in and out of the warp sticks, this time going over the ones that you went under last time and under the ones that you went over. Push this twig down so that it is next to the first one. Continue weaving, alternating the over, under then under, over pattern with each new twig, gently pushing the woven sections downward after each twig is worked in. Stop when the fence is as tall as you want it to be.

If you like, snip off the tops of your warp (up and down) sticks $\frac{1}{2}$" above the last weft (flexible twig). If you want to trim the weft, leave at least 1" sticking out the sides beyond the last warp stick.

Make more fences if your fairy landscape needs them.

3 *plant garden*

Place shells and stones around your fairy landscape—you might want a path of stepping stones, a stone table with stools, or a little bathing pool.

Dampen the soil with a squirt bottle or use your hands to lightly sprinkle about $\frac{3}{4}$ cup water over the whole thing.

Carefully place little chunks of moss around your decorations and gently press them down into the dirt. A variety of colors and textures can make it interesting, but a plain carpet of green is also wonderful. Moss will grow over any bare spots, as long as you water regularly. If you have ferns or grasses, plant them in small holes.

4 *water garden*

Mist or lightly sprinkle more water over your magical garden so that it is damp but not really wet. (Moss doesn't have roots that stick down into the dirt, so it needs regular "rain" from above.) Put your garden near but not right next to a window. To grow well, it needs light but not a lot of sun.

Water your garden about once a week (about $\frac{1}{2}$ cup water) and mist it whenever you like—every day is best because moss likes to be damp. Water droplets from the mist will make your garden and fences glow.

Spend time with your garden—look at it really closely or even with a magnifying glass. It is your own magical place.

Finding Mosses for Your Fairy Garden

MOSSES CAN BE LIKE PEOPLE—THEY ARE VERY TOUGH AND VERY SENSITIVE AT THE SAME TIME. THEY LIVE ALMOST EVERYWHERE, EVEN IN PLACES YOU WOULDN'T EXPECT TO FIND ANY PLANTS GROWING. LOOK FOR THEM AROUND THE BASE OF TREES; ON TREE BARK AND STUMPS; BY THE EDGE OF STONE WALLS OR BUILDINGS IN DAMP, SHADY PLACES; AND IN CRACKS IN THE SIDEWALK. ALWAYS ASK PERMISSION IF YOU ARE COLLECTING MOSSES ON SOMEONE ELSE'S PROPERTY.

To be sure you are giving the moss you choose the best chance of living in your fairy garden, when you pick it, be sure to take a bit of the soil in which it is growing. Or, if it is growing on a rotten tree stump, then take some of the tree stump; if it is growing on a small rock that will fit in your fairy garden, take the moss and rock together (moss that is growing on rocks will not like to be ripped off of one rock and stuck onto the ground or even onto another rock). If desired, you might also take a small fern or grass growing alongside the moss.

Since moss doesn't have roots, it gets most of its nutrients and water through its tiny leaves. Because these leaves are on top, they can dry out really quickly, so remember to mist your garden at least once daily.

Weave a Hideout

ONCE UPON A TIME EVERYONE BUILT THEIR OWN HOUSES USING WHATEVER MATERIALS WERE AROUND THEM. ACTUALLY, IN SOME PARTS OF THE WORLD, PEOPLE STILL DO THIS. IF YOU LIVE WHERE THERE ARE TREES OR BUSHES WITH FLEXIBLE BRANCHES, YOU AND YOUR FRIENDS CAN WEAVE A FABULOUS HIDEOUT.

The hideout shown here was made with branches from birch and maple trees. Willow is also an ideal material for building because it is very flexible and grows in many places. A curious thing about willow is that if you put it into damp ground right after you cut it, it will grow. If you build with willow and don't want a leafy hideout, make sure your big branches have dried out. You can test branches for a hideout by bending them into curves. If they don't crack, they will probably work. Be sure to ask before you cut any branches from someone's property.

To make a hideout, find a place where the dirt is soft but not wet and draw a circle on the ground about 8' across. Ask an adult to use pruning shears to cut 12 or more branches (each about $1\frac{1}{2}$" wide at the base and 10' long) from healthy trees; cut the branches as close to the main branch as possible to avoid hurting the tree. Lay the branches neatly on the ground next to each other. With a piece of rope, tie them all tightly together about 2' from the top. Drag your big bundle to where you drew your circle and stand it up. This is easier with at least 2 people! Spread out the sticks so that the ends go around the circle and are about 2' apart, then push each one into the ground as far as you can—at least a foot. Leave a slightly wider space for a door.

Now weave the walls. You can use almost anything to make the walls as long as it fits between the pieces of the frame—small, flexible branches with leaves, long grasses, flowers, sticks, ferns, or whatever you have at hand. Weave these flexible things over and under and in and out of the sticks that are in the circle. Have fun. There are no rules because you are in charge of how your hideout looks.

friendship
bracelet

THESE COLORFUL BRACELETS ARE MADE using a technique called finger weaving. This technique has been used for centuries by Native Americans to make useful straps and belts. To learn finger weaving, try making these simple friendship bracelets, which can be worn on the wrist or ankle. To make a bracelet or cuff that is wider than the Friendship Bracelet, weave with 8 or 10 strands of yarn. To make a long sash, make each strand of yarn about 8' long. For different effects, try finger weaving with embroidery floss, leather laces, or thick wool yarn.

materials

3 SKEINS #3 PEARL COTTON, IN 3 DIFFERENT COLORS (*available at yarn and craft stores*)

TAPE MEASURE

SCISSORS

PENCIL OR PENCIL-SIZED STICK

BULL-NOSE CLAMP OR CLIPBOARD

1 measure

To figure out how long to weave your bracelet or anklet, using a tape measure, measure your wrist or ankle and double that number.

Cut 3 strands pearl cotton, each a different color. Make each strand about 4' long or tuck the end of the cotton under your toe, measure to your nose and that will be the right length.

Did You Know?
Over two hundred years ago Native Americans taught finger weaving to a group of fur trappers called voyageurs. The voyageurs became famous for their finger-woven straps, which they used for many practical and decorative purposes.

Friends Forever!
Once a friendship bracelet
is tied on, the custom is to
leave it on forever—
or until it falls off
naturally.

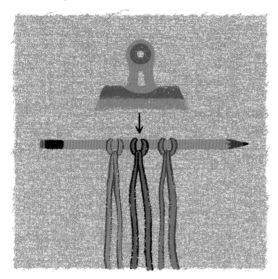

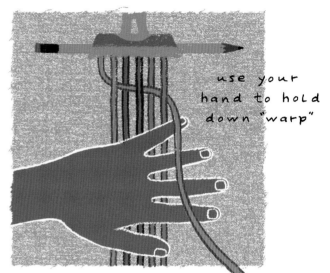

use your hand to hold down "warp"

2 arrange loop knots on pencil

Using the 3 strands of cotton, make 3 loop knots in a row on a pencil. See instuctions for making a loop knot at right.

Put the pencil with the loop knots into the clamp so that the clamp is holding the yarn. You will have 6 strands sticking out—2 of each color.

3 weave first strand

Spread out your 6 strands so that you can see the order they are in. Starting on one

side (you will always start from the same side), pick up one strand and weave it under, over, under, over, under the other strands all the way across. Put your hand on top of the other strands so they don't move and gently pull on the one with which you just wove to tighten it. Set it down and spread out the 6 strands (including the one with which you just wove) neatly in their new order.

4 weave next strand

On the same side you started on, pick up the next strand and weave it across, being sure

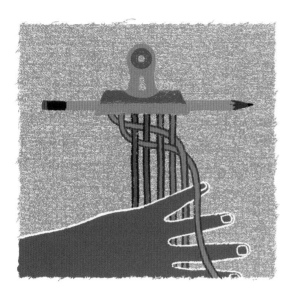

to go under the last strand on the other side (the strand you wove with in the last row). It helps to organize all of the strands each time before starting across with a new one.

Repeat steps 3 and 4 until your bracelet is as long as you want it to be or the yarn is used up. Every inch or so pull on each strand, one at a time, to tighten the weaving.

When ready, remove the yarn from the clamp and the pencil. Knot the ends. Tie your strap around your wrist or ankle (or a friend's) so that it is comfortably loose but will not fall off. Cut off the extra, leaving about 1" fringe.

making a loop knot

*These instructions show
how to make one loop knot.
To make a Friendship Bracelet, make
3 loop knots next to one another.*

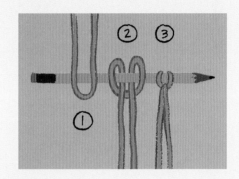

1 *Fold a 4' length of yarn in half and lay the folded loop over a pencil.*

2 *Insert the ends of the yarn through the loop.*

3 *Pull on the ends of the yarn so the loop fits snugly on the pencil.*

weaving *on a* cardboard loom

Some projects are easy to weave with just your hands
as you learned in Chapter 1. But for other projects it is really useful to
have a tool that acts like an extra pair of hands to hold some of the yarn tight.
The tool that was invented for weaving is called a loom, which is a frame that
holds the warp, the up and down part of the weaving, so that your hands are
free to work with the weft, the part that goes from side to side. Looms can be
made out of many materials: They can be made out of fancy wood or plastic
pipe (see page 56), out of a few handy sticks, or even a piece of cardboard,
but all looms do the same basic thing.

For the projects in this chapter you will make cardboard looms.
Cardboard is particularly handy because it is easy to find, inexpensive,
and you can cut it into the perfect size and shape for each project. When you
finish, the weaving comes off of the cardboard. You can save the cardboard
for another project the same size, or just put it into the recycling bin.

Pretty in Pink!
Bryn weaves a Treasure
Pouch on a piece of pretty
pink mat board purchased
at a framing shop.

warping a cardboard loom

IN ORDER TO START WEAVING ON CARDBOARD, YOU NEED TO ATTACH THE WARP YARN, THE UP AND DOWN PART, TO THE CARDBOARD. THIS PROCESS OF PUTTING THE WARP ONTO THE LOOM IS CALLED WARPING. THERE ARE SEVERAL WAYS TO WARP CARDBOARD LOOMS—THE METHOD PRESENTED HERE IS ONE OF THE SIMPLEST.

TO MAKE A CARDBOARD LOOM, YOU NEED A PIECE OF MAT BOARD IN THE SIZE SPECIFIED IN THE PROJECT INSTRUCTIONS, A PENCIL, SCISSORS, MASKING TAPE, AND WARP YARN. THE KIND OF WARP YARN YOU NEED WILL BE SPECIFIED IN YOUR PROJECT INSTRUCTIONS. FOR MORE INFORMATION ABOUT CHOOSING YARN FOR WEAVING, SEE RIGHT.

Steps 1 & 2 *Cut and label cardboard, then cut notches and tabs*

Did You Know?

Yarn is a strand made out of fibers that are twisted together. It can be made out of wool or cotton fiber and even plastic or bamboo. Yarn comes in many different sizes—some yarns are thick and some are thin, some are very strong and some will break even if you just tug on them gently.

1 prepare cardboard

Cut the cardboard to the size specified in the project instructions. Mark the top and the bottom of the cardboard by writing "top" and "bottom." For the projects in this chapter the top and bottom will be at the narrow ends. Pick one side to be the front and one side to be the back. Mark them by writing "Front" or "Back" or putting an "F" or "B" on the appropriate sides.

2 make notches and tabs

At the top of the cardboard, make a mark every $\frac{1}{4}$" on the front side. Make sure that there are an odd number of marks. For the large Treasure Pouch, make 23 marks; for the small Treasure Pouch, make 15 marks. For the Rag Doll Warrior, make 13 marks. At the bottom of the cardboard, make 1 mark about $\frac{1}{8}$" from the front left edge.

Make $\frac{1}{4}$" cuts at the marks. The cuts on this loom are called notches. The cardboard pieces sticking up between the notches are called tabs.

choosing yarn for weaving

You can weave with many different kinds of yarn but here are a few suggestions.

warp yarn   *The yarn that goes up and down is the warp. For most weaving, it is important that the warp yarn is strong. You don't want it to break in the middle of your weaving. To test it, put a piece of warp yarn between your hands and give it a sharp tug; if it breaks, it's not strong enough for weaving. For many projects, kitchen, packing, or kite twine work well.*

weft yarn   *The yarn that goes from side to side is the weft. The weft doesn't have to be nearly as strong as the warp because you do not pull hard on it while weaving. The size of the weft can make a difference in your weaving, however. Some projects call for thick yarn (sometimes called bulky) and some for thinner yarn. If you are going to choose yarn that is different than the yarn called for in the project instructions, it is a good idea to choose one that is similar. All of the projects in this book use high-quality wool or cotton yarn.*

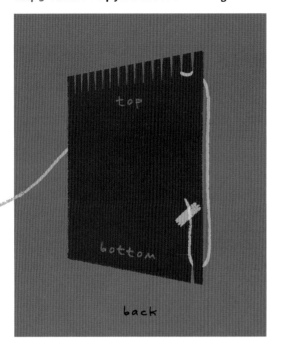

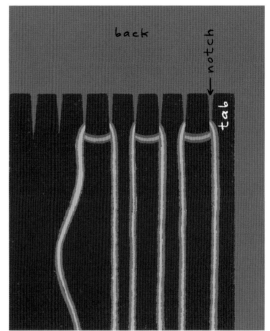

3 attach yarn and start winding

Tape the end of the warp yarn to the back of the loom and bring the yarn to the front, putting it through the bottom notch.

Bring the warp yarn straight up the front of the loom and put it gently through the first notch at the top left. Do not go down the other side. Instead, loop the yarn around the tab between the first and second notches.

4 continue winding warp

Bring the yarn down the front, around the bottom, and up to the top of the back of the loom. As you work, try to keep the warp yarn snug but not so tight that the cardboard bends.

Reverse direction by gently putting the yarn through the first notch again, around the tab on top of the first loop but in the opposite direction, and back out the second notch.

Bring the yarn down the back, around the bottom, and up the front. Reverse direction again by going through the third notch, around the tab, and out the fourth. Every other tab has a loop on both sides. Continue in this pattern: "Down, up, around the tab," "down, up, around the tab" until all the notches are used up.

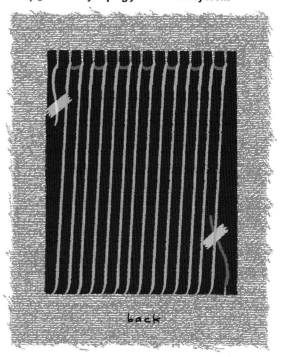

back

5 *finish*

End by coming up the front and through the last notch from front to back. Tape the yarn to the back of the loom, tucking the tape and the end of the yarn under the other warps. There should be an odd number of warp threads if you count the front and back. Do not count or weave the beginning and ending strands where they are taped at the back.

treasure pouch

THESE USEFUL POUCHES ARE AN EASY and fun way to start weaving on a loom. After making your cardboard loom and warping it (putting the warp yarn on it), you simply weave around and around the card-board, practicing your overs and unders as you go. Use the finished pouch to store treasures like colored pencils, coins, dice, jacks, feathers, or a deck of cards.

1 *make and warp your loom*

Follow the instructions starting on page 34 to make a cardboard loom. Make it with 15 notches for a small pouch or 23 notches for a large pouch.

2 *begin weaving*

Thread a yarn needle with a piece of weft (side to side) yarn about 36" long. Starting at one side of the loom front, weave the needle under, over, under, over, all the way across (as shown in the illustration on

materials

CARDBOARD FOR LOOM, 6" × 8" FOR A LARGE POUCH OR 4" × 6" FOR A SMALL POUCH

WARP YARN: STRONG COTTON STRING OR 12/12 SEINE TWINE (*see Sources for Supplies*); ABOUT 12 YARDS FOR LARGE POUCH AND 6 YARDS FOR SMALL ONE.

WEFT YARN: BULKY WOOL YARN, SUCH AS KLIPPAN ASBORYA (*see Sources for Supplies*) IN ONE OR SEVERAL COLORS. ABOUT 75–100 YARDS TOTAL FOR SMALL POUCH AND 125–150 YARDS TOTAL FOR LARGE POUCH.

FORK

YARN NEEDLE

SCISSORS

page 40). Gently pull the yarn so the tail (cut end) is just inside the edge of the card-board and is tucked under the first warp thread.

Step 2 Begin weaving

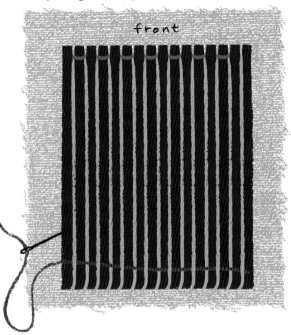

front

3 *turn loom to back and continue*

Turn the loom to the back, picking up the over-under pattern where you left off on the front (if you wove under the last warp on the front, go over the first warp on the back). Weave across the back of the loom the same way that you did on the front except form the weft into the shape of a hill (the steeper, the better). This "hill" is actually called a bubble. Use a fork or your fingers to push the bubbling weft to the bottom of the loom so that it is flat (this is called beating). For more about bubbling and beating, see right. Turn to the front of the loom again and weave across it. This time you will go over the warp (up and down) threads that you went under last time, and under the warp threads that you went over. Remember to bubble and beat the weft yarn well on both sides of the loom.

Continue weaving like this, across the front and then across the back, around and around the loom, until you are $1\frac{1}{2}$" to 2" from the top. If you run out of weft yarn while weaving or want to change colors, attach a new piece following the instructions on page 43.

Step 3 Turn loom to back

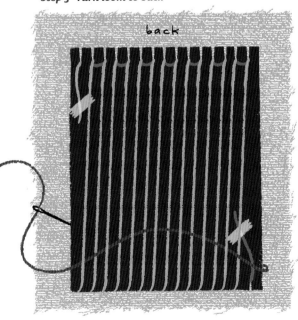

back

bubbling & beating

*Bubbling (or getting enough weft into your weaving) and then beating
(so the weft lies evenly across your loom) are two of the most important things
you can do to make your weaving even and consistent.*

To bubble, instead of weaving from one side of the loom to the other in a straight line, each time you go over and under a group of warp threads, form the weft yarn into a hill shape.

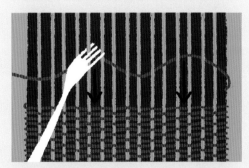

Then, once the hill/bubble has been created, press the hill down firmly with a fork so each strand of yarn lies parallel to the yarn below it. The process of pressing the yarn down is called beating.

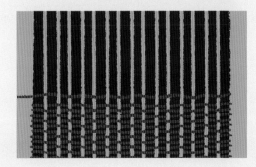

Bubbling and beating are most effective if you make many small hills across the loom, then press each down. To do this, make one big hill that goes all the way across the loom, then press it down in the middle to make 2 smaller hills, then press each of those down in the middle to make 4 still smaller hills and so on until each hill disappears and the weft lies evenly across the loom.

Step 4 *Weave slits for drawstring*

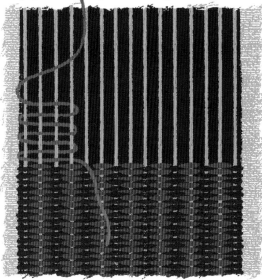

Step 4 *Weave in tails*

weave
in
end
tail

weave in
start tail

4 *weave slits for drawstring*

To make slits for the drawstring, you need to stop weaving around the whole loom and, instead, weave back and forth on only 3 or 4 warp threads at a time until you have created a series of $3/4$" rectangles, as follows:

Thread about 12" yarn onto your needle. Instead of weaving the end in, leave a 4" tail at the beginning. Weave back and forth over a group of 3 or 4 warp threads until your rectangle measures $3/4$" tall after it has been beaten well. Bury the end of the yarn into the weaving by pushing the needle down into the already woven part for about an inch, bringing it out and pulling the yarn

tight. Cut the yarn where it comes out of the weaving. Thread the end that you left hanging at the beginning of the rectangle onto the needle and bury it down into the already woven part, cutting it where it emerges.

Weave more rectangles with other groups of 3 or 4 warp threads until the warps are all used up and you have a series of woven rectangles with slits between them. The pouch will close more smoothly if there are the same number of rectangles on both sides of the loom. The width of the individual rectangles can vary.

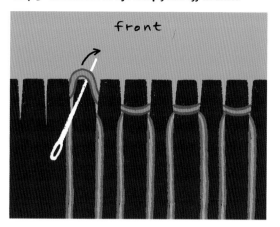

front

5 *weave top of bag*

Return to weaving around the loom as you did before you started making the slits for the drawstring until you can't squeeze in any more rows. Firmly press down the parts that are already woven to make it easier to fit in more rows. Sometimes, at the very end, you have to weave under one warp at a time because there is hardly any room for your needle between the weaving and the notches. The more rows you can fit in, the sturdier your pouch will be.

When you have woven as many rows as will fit in, use your needle to lift the loops of warp yarn off the notches at the top. Pull the cardboard loom out of the middle of your weaving to release your pouch.

attaching a new piece of weft yarn

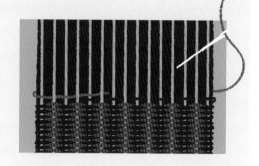

While you are weaving, at some point, you are bound to run out of weft yarn or want to change colors. Fortunately, it's very easy to attach a new piece of yarn to your work. Simply weave until your yarn is used up. Then, thread a new length of yarn onto your needle—the same or a different color. Weave this new piece in the same direction as the last piece, overlapping the new weft with the old one for an inch or so.

Pick up the warp end that was taped to the cardboard and thread it onto your needle. Bury it into the woven part of your pouch and cut off the end.

6 *finish*

Wash and full your bag with as much agitation as you can (see page 109). Set the bag aside to dry.

While the bag is drying, make 2 twisted cords (in the same or different colors) to use as drawstrings following the instructions at right. Thread the 2 cords through the pouch slits so that the 2 ends of one cord stick out one side and the 2 ends of the other cord stick out the opposite side. Knot the ends together. Pull the 2 opposing knots and your pouch will close.

Step 6 *Close bag with twisted cord*

Tie your pouch to your belt loop to keep your hands free—to look in another pouch, pick flowers, whatever you like.

twisted cord & fringe

Twisted cord is strong, thick cord made of strands of thinner yarn twisted together. You can use it to make a drawstring, hair tie, friendship bracelet, or even for tidying up fringe at the end of scarves, blankets, or other woven fabrics.

1 For a twisted cord (as for Treasure Pouch), cut 4 pieces weft yarn, each about 3' long. Tape or clamp the group of 4 ends of yarn to something solid, such as a chair.

2 Twist 2 of the strands of yarn together in the same direction until they are so twisted that they start to twist back on themselves. Give to a friend to hold so it doesn't untwist.

3 Twist the other 2 strands of yarn together in the same direction as the first 2 strands.

4 Being careful not to lose any twist, knot the ends of the 2 twisted sections together and carefully allow them to twist back around each other.

For twisted fringe (as for the Chenille Scarf, page 102, and West African Blanket, page 106), put something heavy on top of your woven fabric and repeat steps 2 through 4 with groups of the warp threads that stick out of the fabric.

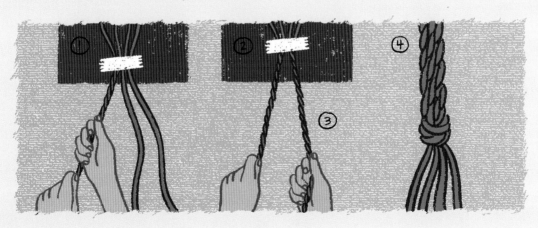

rag doll *warriors*

IN JAPAN, THE FIFTH OF MAY IS A special day when people celebrate the future health, happiness, and success of children. It is a day filled with delicious food, kite-flying, and lots of fancy decorations. In the midst of it all, everyone displays their Hina-Ningyo and Gogatsu-Ningyo, special warrior dolls made by the children as symbols of their courage, strength, and happiness.

You, too, can make a doll of your own to celebrate your courage, happiness, and skill as a weaver. When you weave your doll using strips of cloth instead of yarn for weft, the side to side part of the weaving, it becomes extra-special. You can buy cloth in many colors to make into these strips, or you can use old clothes that are nearly worn out. These "rag" strips bring new life to the old clothes and also bring your particular strengths, the magic of you, to your doll.

materials

1 (3½" × 8") CARDBOARD LOOM WITH 13 NOTCHES (*see page 34*)

ABOUT 6 YARDS STRONG COTTON STRING OR 12/12 SEINE TWINE (*see Sources for Supplies*), FOR WARP

ASSORTMENT OF OLD CLOTHES, SHEETS, OR OTHER FABRIC, TO BE CUT INTO RAG STRIPS FOR THE BODY AND CLOTHES. YOU WILL NEED 2 OR 3 DIFFERENT COLORS, EACH ABOUT 18" TO 24" SQUARE.

A FEW YARDS BULKY YARN, SUCH AS BROWN SHEEP LAMB'S PRIDE BULKY (*see Sources for Supplies*), FOR HAIR

FORK

YARN NEEDLE

SCISSORS

FABRIC SCRAPS OR A FEW HANDFULS OF POLYESTER STUFFING, FOR STUFFING DOLL

Doll Power!

Weave dolls to represent you and your friends and to celebrate how good you feel when you are together.

making rag strips

Using favorite but worn-out clothing to make something new is irresistible to people who love fabric; it is also a sensible way to save the parts that are still in good shape.

Often people use rag strips to make weft for rag rugs. You can make your rag strips out of almost any cloth. If you don't have a collection of old clothes to choose from, look for some at thrift stores. You can also buy remnants (leftover bits) of cloth at fabric stores, or "fat quarters" at quilting stores. Fat quarters are small squares or rectangles of fabric left over from bigger pieces of fabric that have been cut.

To create the strips needed for the Rag Doll Warrior, cut or tear your fabric into pieces about 18" to 36" long and $\frac{1}{2}$" wide. You can cut the strips with scissors or, with certain fabric, you can snip the edge and then tear. Sometimes you have to pull hard. Cut strips are tidier, but torn strips are faster. Try both and see which you like better.

1 warp loom and prepare rag strips

Warp your loom following the instructions starting on page 34. Choose fabric for the skirt, torso and arms, and head, and cut or tear into strips about $\frac{1}{2}$" wide and no longer than 36", following the instructions at left.

2 weave skirt

Starting at the bottom of the loom, weave around the loom with the rag strips you've chosen for the skirt, following Steps 2 and 3 for the Treasure Pouch (see page 38). Remember to bubble your weft yarn well (see page 41) and then beat or push each row tightly down on top of the row before so that you cannot see the warp. Stop weaving when you have woven about halfway up the loom. When you reach the end of a strip, start with another one following the instructions on page 43.

3 weave torso and arms

Choose rag strips for the torso (or continue with the same fabric you used for the skirt) and weave around with these fabric strips for about $1\frac{1}{2}$".

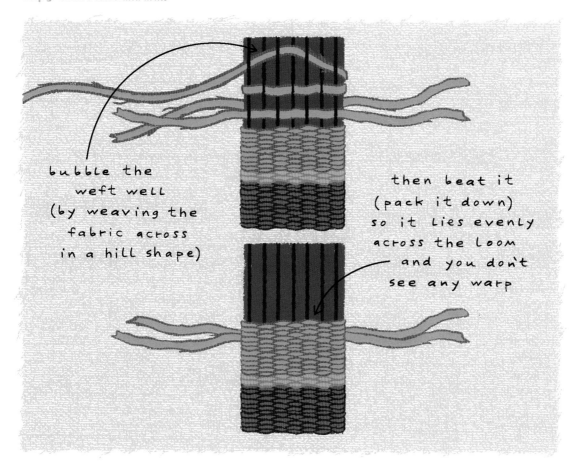

bubble the
weft well
(by weaving the
fabric across
in a hill shape)

then beat it
(pack it down)
so it lies evenly
across the loom
and you don't
see any warp

Cut twelve 15" rag strips for the arms. Weave one of these strips across the front of the loom and another one across the back of the loom, leaving about 6" hanging on each side.

Weave twice around as usual with the main body rag strips, bubbling and beating well.

Repeat at least 6 times so you end up with at least 12 or more individual strips of rags hanging off each side of the loom. At this point, there should be about 2" of warp left for the head.

Ghiordes knots

*A Ghiordes (rhymes with forties) knot is not really a knot at all.
It is a piece of cut yarn that is looped around the warp and then held in place by the
rows of weaving. Ghiordes knots are used to create the hair on the Rag Doll Warrior.
They're also used to create the Magic Carpets on page 110.*

A Ghiordes knot is made in 3 steps

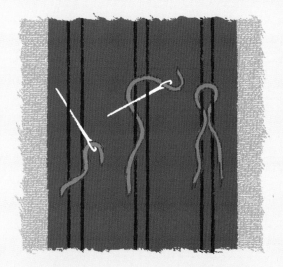

**Shown here are 2 rows weaving,
2 Ghiordes knots, 2 rows weaving**

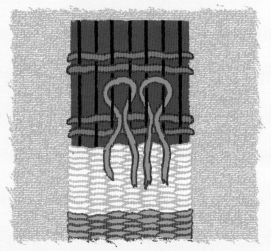

1   Thread about 24" of yarn onto a needle. Pick 2 warp threads where you want your first knot to appear. Put the needle under the left warp thread from right to left, leaving a tail that is 2" to 3" long if you are making the doll ($\frac{1}{2}$" long if you are making the Magic Carpet on page 110).

2   Bring the needle over the top of both warp threads and back under the right warp thread, coming out where the needle first went in.

3   Cut the end to match the other end of the same piece of yarn.

4 weave head and hair

Choose rag strips for the face/head/skin color and weave around twice.

Thread some yarn for the hair onto a yarn needle and weave a row of Ghiordes knots across the back of the loom where the back of the head will be, leaving the hair strands as long as you want them. To learn how to make Ghiordes knots, see left.

Weave around twice more.

Weave another row of Ghiordes knots across the back.

Repeat until you can't squeeze in any more rows. To finish hair, weave a row of knots across the back and the front of the loom (the knots on the front are for bangs). Weave all the way around the loom once or twice more to hold the knots in place.

5 finish doll

Use your needle to pry the loops off of the notches at the top of the loom (as shown in the Treasure Pouch instructions on page 43). Pull out the cardboard (this is sometimes easier if you bend the cardboard to make it smaller).

Stuff the doll through the head and down into the body with more rags or polyester filling, until firm but not too hard.

Braid the arms (so you have one braid on each side of body) and use scraps of yarn or fabric to secure the ends of the braids at the wrists.

Sew the top of the head closed with a piece of hair yarn or a rag strip the same color as the face. Knot the hair in front to the hair in back to cover up the seam on top of the head. Trim or style the hair as you like.

Glorious Colors from Natural Dyes

We live in a colorful world full of beautiful plants, flowers, trees, and insects, some of which contain special dye substances that we can use to dye weaving yarn. Following are instructions for dyeing wool with onion skins to create yellowish brown colors and with cochineal (a kind of dried bug) and madder (a plant root) to create pink and reddish orange colors. The dye in onion skins sticks to wool naturally when you simmer them together, but madder and cochineal need the help of a naturally occurring substance called a mordant in order to adhere. This type of dyeing requires the use of a stove and very hot water, so make sure that an adult is available to help when necessary.

materials

NEWSPAPER OR DROP CLOTH, TO COVER
THE FLOOR AND COUNTERS

1 GALLON OR LARGER STAINLESS-STEEL
OR ENAMEL POT, CLEANED AND USED
ONLY FOR DYEING

ABOUT 3 QUARTS WARM WATER

POTHOLDERS

RUBBER GLOVES

STICK OR SPOON, FOR STIRRING (USED
ONLY FOR DYEING)

ABOUT 8 OUNCES ONION SKINS (*available from produce manager at most grocery stores*)

4 OUNCES CLEAN, UNDYED, LIGHT-
COLORED WOOL YARN WOUND INTO
AN OPEN SKEIN (*see page 55*)

dyeing with onion skins

Note that these instructions will work when dyeing wool yarn or fabric only.

1   extract dye

Put onion skins and water into pot and bring to a boil. Lower heat and simmer about 1 hour or until water is yellowish brown and onion skins are mushy and limp.

2   wash yarn

While dye is being extracted from onions, wash yarn following directions for Washing and Fulling on page 109; do not agitate yarn.

3 dye yarn

When ready, gently place the wet, clean yarn into pot with hot dye liquid. Stir gently but briefly and then let liquid slowly heat up to a low simmer, until you can see steam and there are tiny bubbles in the water (try not to let the liquid boil). Simmer for about an hour, giving the pot a short gentle stir every 10 minutes or so. After an hour, turn off heat and let yarn cool in pot until an adult tests it and tells you that you will be able to handle it without burning yourself, about 1 hour.

4 rinse and dry

While yarn is cooling in pot, fill a sink or tub with warm water. Squeeze excess dye and onion skins out of yarn and transfer to the tub. Wash and rinse gently (see page 109). Squeeze out as much water as you can after the last rinse and hang yarn to dry where it can drip. If desired, go outside, hold skein of yarn at end of your arm, and twirl it as fast as you can. The yarn dries faster if you do this but sprays everything and everyone around with water droplets! When yarn is dry, shake skein to remove any onion skin sticking to it.

Dyeing with natural dyes is an inexact science. The color you get depends on the nature of the particular batch of dye you are using as well as your water and other environmental factors on dye day.

Shown here from top to bottom are skeins of yarn dyed with madder root, dried cochineal, and onion skins. The ball of yarn to the right is undyed. To dye it, it first needs to be wound into a skein (see page 55).

dyeing with cochineal and madder

These instructions call for dye that has been extracted from its plant or animal source and then made into a powder.

1 mordant yarn

Wash yarn following directions for Washing and Fulling on page 111; do not agitate. Put alum in yogurt container. Add $\frac{1}{2}$ cup hot water; stir to dissolve. Put 3 quarts warm water and dissolved alum into pot of water; stir well. Add wet yarn. Slowly, over about 30 minutes, bring temperature up to a simmer. Simmer about 1 hour, stirring gently every 10 minutes. Remove pot from heat and let yarn cool in pot for several hours. Rinse yarn in tub of warm water and squeeze well.

2 dye yarn

Put dye extract powder into plastic container, add about 1 tablespoon hot or boiling water, and stir to make paste. Add $\frac{1}{2}$ cup hot water and stir again. Put 3 quarts warm water and the dissolved dye into the dye pot. Stir well. Add rinsed, mordanted yarn to pot. Slowly, over about 60 minutes, bring temperature up to a simmer. Simmer 30 to 45 minutes, stirring gently every 10 minutes. Remove pot from heat and allow yarn to cool for several hours. Wash and rinse yarn following step 4 on page 53.

materials

ALL MATERIALS LISTED FOR ONION-SKIN DYEING (*see page 52*), PLUS THE FOLLOWING:

SMALL PLASTIC CONTAINER, SUCH AS EMPTY YOGURT CONTAINER

*ALUM——2 TEASPOONS PER 4 OUNCES YARN (*available in spice section of grocery stores*)

*DYE MATERIAL (CHOOSE ONE AT A TIME)

COCHINEAL EXTRACT FOR PINK—— $\frac{1}{4}$ TEASPOON FOR LIGHT COLOR, $\frac{1}{2}$ TEASPOON FOR DARK

MADDER EXTRACT FOR RED-ORANGE—— $\frac{1}{2}$ TEASPOON FOR LIGHT COLOR, 1 TEASPOON FOR DARK

*THESE DYEING MATERIALS ARE SOLD AT DYE SUPPLY STORES (*see Sources for Supplies*).

winding yarn

Sometimes yarn comes in a ball that unwinds easily.
Sometimes, it comes in the shape of a coil or a figure 8, called a skein (rhymes with rain).
Depending on what you want to do with the yarn, you may need to rewind it.

winding skein of yarn into ball

To rewind a skein into a ball (if you try to weave from a skein, your yarn will end up all knotted up), untwist the figure 8 so you have one big coil. Place coil around back of a chair or a friend's outstretched arms and, with scissors, cut any short pieces of yarn holding individual strands of yarn together. Find one end of the yarn and begin winding it around your fingers loosely. After winding about 20 times in one direction, shift the yarn on your fingers and wind in another direction. Continue until you have one big ball.

winding ball of yarn into skein

To rewind a ball into a skein (if you want to dye the yarn, for example), wrap it around the arms of a friend or a chair in a big continuous loop. Before you take it off, tie pieces of string loosely around it in 4 places so it doesn't get tangled.

beginning
on a pipe loom

You have already learned that weaving is a simple process
and for it to work well there are 2 things that have to happen.
First, the up and down strands (the warp) have to be organized and
kept tight. Second, the weaver needs some way to interlace the side to
side strands (the weft) with that warp. So far you have made your weft go
over and under one warp at a time. Now you will use a loom that allows
you to lift groups of threads and go under them all at once.
In fact, you're going to make a loom yourself.

The loom you are going to make—called a pipe loom—
is constructed out of plumbing parts and can be used for many different
weaving techniques. A weaver named Archie Brennan thought up the original
concept for this type of loom with pipes. In this book, you use the pipe loom
to make shoelaces, a scarf, a blanket, and even small carpets.

Wandering Weaver!
**Because a pipe loom is lightweight
and portable, you can carry it around
with you and weave wherever you are—
on your front porch, at a friend's house,
or even in a canoe.**

making a pipe loom

MOST OF THE PARTS YOU NEED TO MAKE A PIPE LOOM ARE SOLD AT HARDWARE STORES. THE PVC PIPE IS VERY CHEAP, SO YOU DON'T HAVE TO SPEND MUCH MONEY AT ALL TO MAKE A GREAT LOOM. ASK A WORKER THERE TO CUT PVC PIPE INTO THE SIZES ON THE LIST BELOW USING A PVC PIPE CUTTER (NOT A HACKSAW).

materials

10' SECTION $^3/_4$" PVC PIPE, CUT INTO:
- 2 20" PIECES
- 3 14" PIECES
- 1 13$^3/_4$" PIECE
- 2 8" PIECES
- 2 2" PIECES

3' SECTION $^3/_4$" PVC PIPE, CUT INTO:
- 2 2" PIECES
- 4 8" PIECES

PIPE FITTINGS
- 6 $^3/_4$" × $^3/_4$" × $^3/_4$" T'S
- 4 $^3/_4$" 90-DEGREE ELBOWS
- 2 1" × 1" × $^3/_4$" T'S

1"-DIAMETER WOODEN DOWEL, CUT AS FOLLOWS:
- 1 13" PIECE
- 1 11" PIECE

2 CAMPING OR SLEEPING BAG STRAPS, AT LEAST 2' LONG WITH STRONG, EASY-TO-USE BUCKLES (AVAILABLE AT SPORTING-GOODS STORES)

1 ROLL APPROXIMATELY 1"-WIDE MASKING TAPE

APPROXIMATELY 10 6" × $^3/_4$" CRAFT STICKS

assemble pipe loom

Putting your loom together is a straightforward job. As you put the pieces together, label each part neatly with a permanent marker; this will make the warping and weaving instructions easier to follow. Refer to the illustrations as you build your loom.

1 Locate all of the pieces on the materials list and lay them out in a big open space where you can comfortably assemble your loom. Keep all of the same types of pieces together at this point—for example, keep all of the 8" pieces of PVC pipe together.

2 Make the Side Bars: Use one of the smaller T's ($^3/_4$") to connect a 20" piece of pipe to an 8" piece of pipe lengthwise, end to end. Make another one. These 29"-long pieces are your side bars. Label them.

Your pipe loom——in pieces

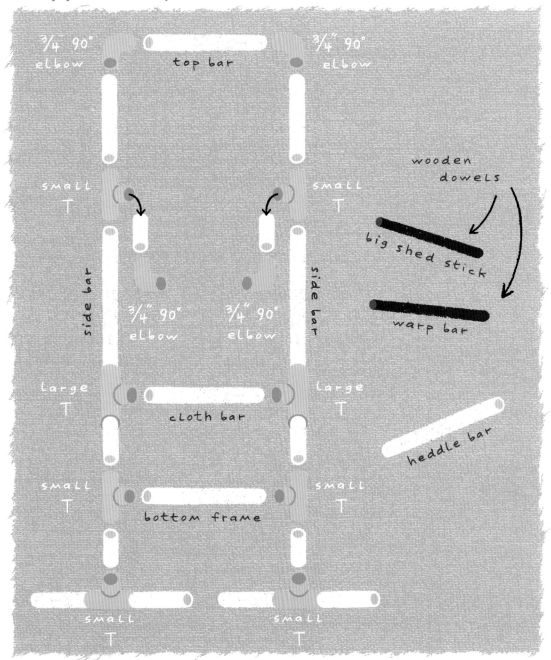

¾" 90°
elbow

top bar

¾" 90°
elbow

small
T

small
T

wooden
dowels

side bar

¾" 90°
elbow

¾" 90°
elbow

side bar

big shed stick

warp bar

large
T

cloth bar

large
T

heddle bar

small
T

small
T

bottom frame

small
T

small
T

Your pipe loom—assembled

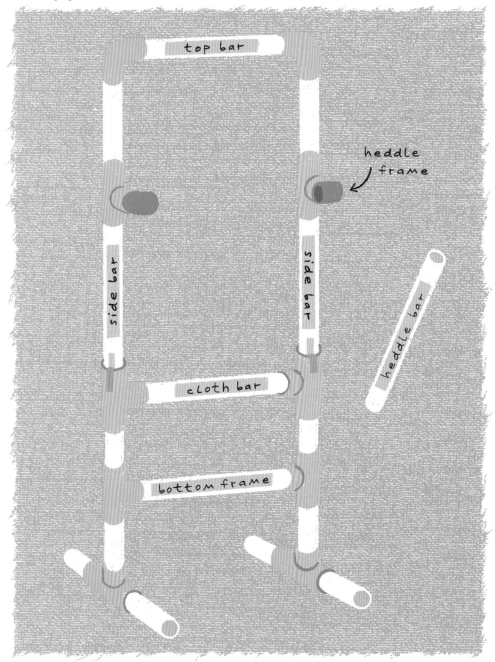

top bar

heddle frame

side bar

side bar

heddle bar

cloth bar

bottom frame

3 Make the Top Bar: Put a $^3/_4$" elbow on each end of one of the 14" pieces of pipe. This is your top bar. Label it.

4 Connect the Side Bars to the Top Bar: Put the top bar elbows onto the ends of the 8" pieces of pipe on the side bars. The whole frame will look like an upside down U at this point.

5 Make the Cloth Bar: Put the small opening of the 1" × 1" × $^3/_4$" T's on to both ends of the 13$^3/_4$" piece of $^3/_4$" pipe. Label it.

6 Slide the cloth bar onto the open ends of the side bars (the open end of the U).

7 Make the Bottom Frame Bar: Put one $^3/_4$" T on each end of one of the 14" pieces of pipe. This is your bottom frame bar. Label it.

8 Put the bottom frame bar onto the open ends of the side bars. The cloth bar can now slide up and down the side bars without falling off.

9 Make Feet: Put a 2" piece of pipe into the shortest segment of one $^3/_4$" T. Repeat with

the remaining $^3/_4$" T and 2" piece of pipe. Put an 8" piece of pipe in each of the open ends of each T. Put the 2" piece of pipe into each T on the end of the bottom frame bar. You can now stand your loom on its feet.

10 Make the Heddle Frame: Put the last 2 elbows onto one end of each of the two 2" pieces of pipe. Put the pieces of pipe you just assembled into the T's that stick out in the middle of the side bars so that the open holes of the elbow joints are facing each other. Label it.

11 Heddle Bar: There should be one 14" piece left. It is the heddle bar. Label it and set it aside until later.

12 Warp Bar and Big Shed Stick: The 11" piece of dowel is your big shed stick. The 13" piece of dowel is your warp bar. Label them and set aside until later (they are both used for projects in Chapter 4).

When everything is in its place and your loom looks like the illustration at left, push firmly on every joint to make sure that your loom is as solid as it can be.

warping a pipe loom—method 1

MOST WARPING TAKES LONGER TO DESCRIBE THAN TO DO—IT IS REALLY JUST A SERIES OF SMALL STEPS. MANY WEAVERS LOOK FORWARD TO WARPING BECAUSE IT MARKS THE BEGINNING OF A NEW PROJECT. SOME PEOPLE CALL THE PROCESS OF WARPING "DRESSING THE LOOM." THE WARPING METHOD SHOWN HERE WORKS FOR ALL OF THE PROJECTS IN THIS CHAPTER. (TO MAKE THE WARPING EASIER THE FIRST FEW TIMES, MAKE A PHOTOCOPY OF THE ILLUSTRATION ON PAGE 63 AND PLACE IT NEXT TO PAGE 64 SO YOU DON'T HAVE TO FLIP PAGES BACK AND FORTH.) A SECOND WARPING METHOD IS SHOWN IN THE NEXT CHAPTER.

materials

ASSEMBLED LOOM; YOU WILL NOT NEED THE WARP BAR OR THE BIG SHED STICK

RULER

PEN OR MARKER

CLOTHESPIN OR STRONG CLIP

WARP AND WEFT YARN— EACH PROJECT WILL TELL YOU WHAT YARN TO USE AND HOW MUCH

STRONG COTTON STRING, SUCH AS KITCHEN STRING, FOR HEDDLES

SCISSORS

6" × 6" PIECE CARDBOARD

1 mark center

Put a piece of tape all the way across the front of the top bar and all the way across the front of the cloth bar (be careful not to cover up the name you wrote on each part). Measure to the center and make a dark line on the tape at the center of each taped bar. The center of your loom will be the center of your weaving. Make slightly smaller marks 1" and 2" on both sides of your center mark.

2 position and secure movable cloth bar

Lay the loom on its back (so the heddle frame is facing up) on the floor. Put your straps around the cloth bar and bottom frame bar and put the strap ends through

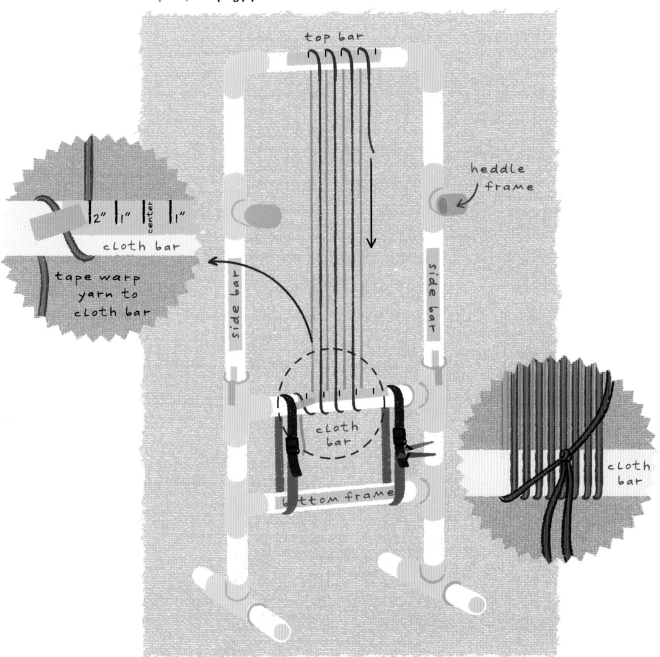

top bar

heddle frame

side bar

side bar

2" 1" center 1"

cloth bar

tape warp yarn to cloth bar

cloth bar

bottom frame

cloth bar

the buckles. Tighten the straps evenly so that when you push up on the cloth bar there is about 4" between the 2 bars (the cloth bar and the bottom frame) all the way across. Push the cloth bar up against the straps and keep it in this position by taping it to the side bars.

3 attach warp to cloth bar

Clip the clothespin or strong clip to one of the straps at the bottom. This can be used to hold the tension on your warp if you have to stop in the middle of winding your warp. Then tape the end of the warp yarn to the cloth bar so that it wraps under the bar and then passes over the top (see illustration on page 63). It should be taped about 1" to the left side of the center mark.

4 wind on warp

You will be making a continuous loop around the cloth bar and top bar. Try to keep the tension on the warp firm and even, not floppy. Refer to the illustration on page 63 as you wind.

Beginning where the yarn is taped to the bottom of the cloth bar, bring the yarn all the way up the back and over the top bar (back to front). Then bring the yarn down and under the cloth bar (front to back). When you are winding on the warp, lay each warp next to the one before and do not let the warp strands cross over each other. Repeat until you have the number of warp ends called for in your project (for more about warp ends, see page 67). End at the bottom by clipping the end of the yarn to the clothespin or clamp. If necessary, adjust the tension so it is firm. If the yarn is loose, pull it to make it tight.

Make sure your warp is centered on the top bar and cloth bar. Remove the beginning and ends of the yarn from the tape and the clip and knot them together securely. These ends will cross over the other warps when you tie them. Cut the tails of yarn hanging from the knot so they are about 2" long.

5 check warp

Remove the tape that attaches the cloth bar to the side bars and remove the clothespin that is clipped to the strap. Check the tension again. Your warp should feel tight like a trampoline. If it isn't, tighten the straps a

Your warp is a big loop, with half of it on the front of your loom and half on the back. You will do all of your weaving on the part in front. As you weave you will rotate the warp so that the woven part moves to the back for storage and the empty warp on the back moves to the front to be woven.

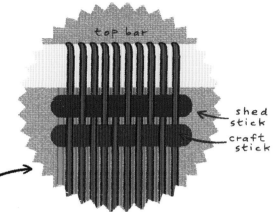

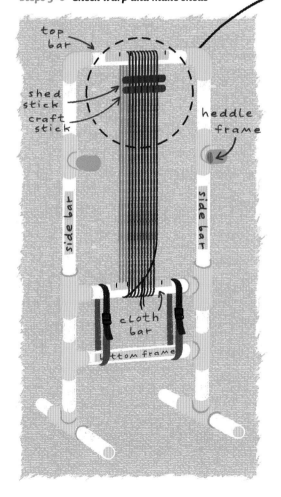

6   *make sheds*

One of the things that makes this loom so useful is that you can easily lift a whole group of warp threads at one time. This makes a space between the ones that are up (the unders) and the ones that are down (the overs). This space is called a shed.

Just below where the warp comes over the top bar on the front of your loom, weave a craft stick under and over all the warp threads. The craft stick is now your shed stick; make sure the shed stick is centered on the warp.

Weave a second craft stick just below the first, going over the unders and under the overs.

65

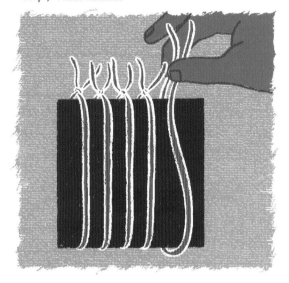

Tie each piece of string around the cardboard as shown at left. Make sure to tie the string tight but don't bend the cardboard! Cut off extra string above the knot. Store the heddles on the cardboard until needed.

8 install heddles

Slide the lower craft stick (not the shed stick) down so it is slightly below the heddle frame. Turn the craft stick on its side so it separates the warp threads. Take a heddle off the cardboard, loop it around the first warp thread in front so it surrounds the warp thread in a U-shape with the opening at the front. Slide the heddle bar into the loops of the heddle. It can be helpful to have someone else hold the heddle bar while you put the heddle on it.

Continue to put the remaining heddles on each of the raised warp threads and feed them onto the heddle bar. Remove the craft stick when all of the heddles are on the heddle bar, then put the ends of the heddle bar into the elbows on the heddle bar frame (the heddle bar is shown in the frame on the illustration on page 68). The heddles on the bar will hold half of the warp threads in the "up" position.

7 make heddles

Heddles are loops of string that lift warp threads. They should all be the same size (weaving is really difficult if they are not). To make them, first cut out a 6" square of cardboard. Then cut an 18" piece of strong cotton string for each heddle you need (your project instructions tell you how many heddles to make; for example, if you're making the shoelaces on page 74, you need 5 heddles.) It is helpful if the string you use to make the heddles is a different color than the yarn you are using to weave.

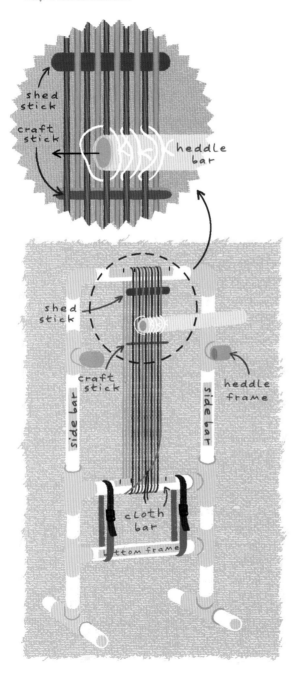

shed
stick

craft
stick

heddle
bar

shed
stick

craft
stick

heddle
frame

side bar

side bar

cloth
bar

bottom frame

loom set-up

At the beginning of each pipe-loom project is a list of important information about how your warp should look when you've finished winding it on the loom.

Total Warp Ends: number of warp ends (strands) on the front of the loom.

Sett: number of ends (strands) per inch, or e.p.i.

Width on Loom: number of inches wide your warp should be before you start weaving.

These pieces of information are directly related both to each other and to how your final project will look and feel. If you like math you will see that:

Width on Loom × Sett = Total Warp Ends

or

Total Warp Ends ÷ Sett = Width on Loom

For example, a stiff rug woven with thick wool might have 100 total warp ends and a sett of 4 e.p.i., which means it will be 25" wide. A super-soft, fine-silk scarf might have 100 total warp ends with a sett of 25 e.p.i., which means it will be 4" wide.

9 test sheds

A shed is the space between warps that are up (the ones that your weft yarn will go under) and warps that are down (the ones that your weft yarn will go over). The heddles you just made pull up half of the warps so there is an open space called the open shed. Every other row, however, you will need to go over the warps that are held up by the heddles and under the warps that are down. You will use your shed stick (the craft stick at the top of the loom) to lift the warps that are down above the ones that are up, making a new shed (or space), as follows:

Slide the shed stick down to the heddles and pull it toward the heddle bar, lifting the threads at the back. Try to do this with one hand because when you are weaving you will need the other hand for the weft (side to side) yarn. To make sure the shed stick cannot accidentally slide out of the warp, tape a piece of string around the front of it as shown at top right.

If the shed is hard to open, try strumming the warp threads with your fingers (as if you are playing a guitar) in case they are stuck together or try adjusting the tension—it could be too tight or too loose.

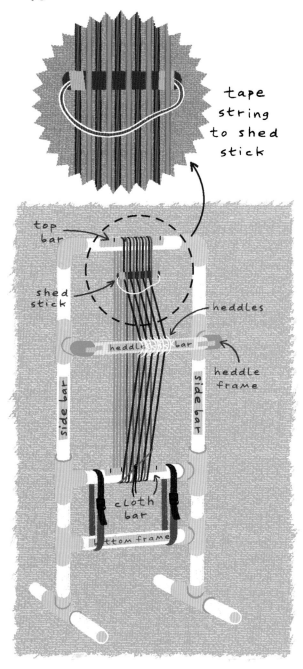

tape string to shed stick

top bar

shed stick

heddles

heddle bar

heddle frame

side bar

side bar

cloth bar

bottom frame

10 weave in spacers

Before you can weave with yarn, you will need to make the warp smooth and even at the bottom of the loom. To do this, weave 3 craft sticks into alternate sheds for spacers, as follows:

Put the first craft stick into the shed that is currently open just below where the heddles lift the warp. Push it down as far as it will go toward the cloth bar.

Open the other shed (which closes the first shed) by pulling the shed stick down and toward the heddle bar. Put the second craft stick into the shed that is open now. Push the second craft stick down as far as it will go toward the first.

Slide the shed stick back to the top of the loom so that the shed that was open when you started is open again. Slide in the third craft stick. Check to make sure that the warp threads alternate going over and under the sticks. The first and third will be the same; the second will be different.

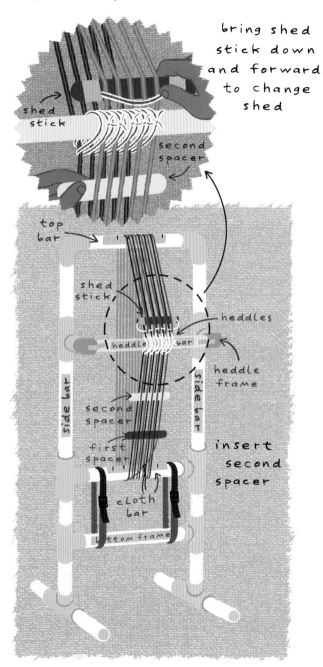

bring shed stick down and forward to change shed

shed stick

second spacer

top bar

shed stick

heddles

heddle bar

heddle frame

side bar

side bar

second spacer

insert second spacer

first spacer

cloth bar

bottom frame

Pipe loom—assembled, warped, and ready for weaving

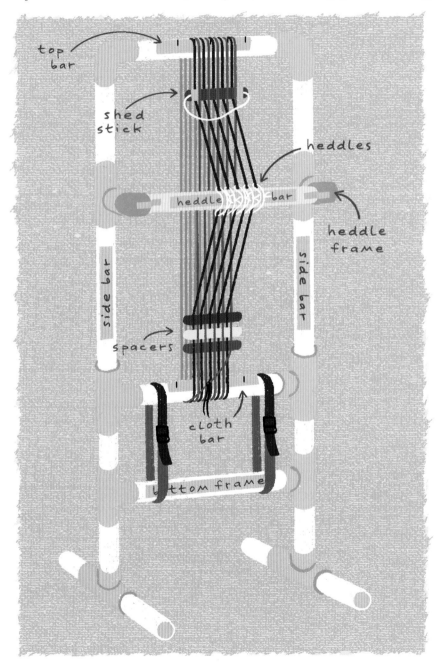

top bar

shed stick

heddles

heddle bar

heddle frame

side bar

side bar

spacers

cloth bar

bottom frame

shuttles

Now that your loom is assembled and warped, you need only one more tool to start weaving. It is called a shuttle. It holds long pieces of weft yarn while you weave with it. First you wind the yarn onto the shuttle and then you unwind it, a little at a time, as you weave. There are many kinds of shuttles. The simplest is an X-shaped stick shuttle. To make one, you need 2 craft sticks and masking tape.

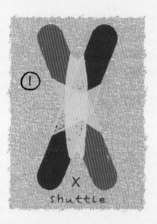

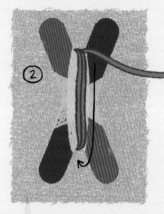

1   Make a flattened X with 2 of your sticks. Tape them together in that shape at the point where the sticks meet by wrapping one piece of tape from top to bottom and one piece of tape from side to side. Keep your shuttle tall and thin so it can easily pass through the open shed.

2   To wind the weft yarn around the shuttle, hold the tail of the weft yarn against the middle of the shuttle, then wind around and around longways until it gets bulky. Let go of the tail as soon as it is held on by the rest of the yarn. Cut or break the yarn when the shuttle is full.

fixing a broken warp thread

Sometimes your warp breaks. There are several reasons why this happens, but usually it is because the yarn isn't strong enough for the tension put on it by your loom. Sometimes a warp thread doesn't break, but it accidentally gets cut. In either case, the solution is the same. You will need a piece of warp yarn about 60" long, a yarn needle, a straight pin, and scissors to make the fix.

1 The broken warp will have 2 ends—one that goes up to the unwoven warp and another that goes down into the fabric that you are weaving. Let the end that is already woven into the fabric drop down behind the fabric. Find the unwoven end and firmly knot it to the new piece of yarn at the beginning of the warp (by the spacers). Cut off any extra.

2 Bring the free end of the new yarn to where you are weaving, making sure that it is in the same position as the broken yarn—it will go under the cloth bar, up the back of the loom, over the top bar, and either over the shed stick and straight to the weaving, or under the shed stick and through a heddle.

3 Thread the yarn onto a needle and sew it down into the weaving right next to the broken end. Bring it out 2" to 3" from where you started. Attach a straight pin to the weaving just below the point where your yarn emerges from the fabric so that it is perpendicular to the warp. Gently pull on the new warp yarn until it is about as tight as the rest of the warp and wrap it in a figure 8 around the pin—as many times as will fit on the pin. This should hold the tension until you have finished weaving.

When you take the weaving off of the loom, remove the pin. Cut off the excess yarn that you wound around the pin, as well as the broken piece and the new end where it emerges from the fabric.

Step 1 **Attach new piece of warp yarn with firm knot**

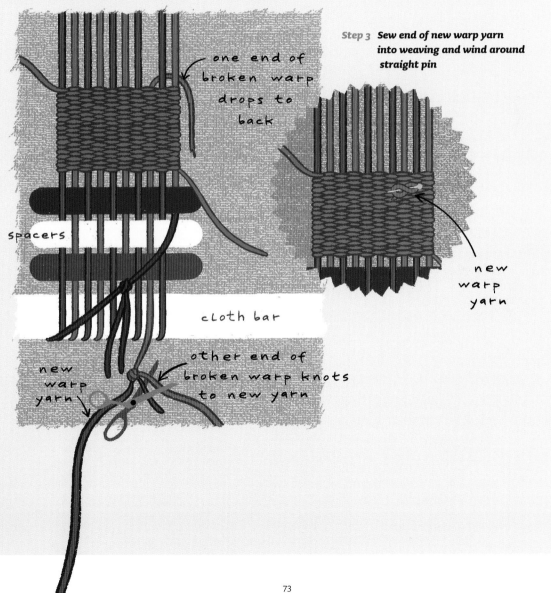

one end of broken warp drops to back

spacers

cloth bar

new warp yarn

other end of broken warp knots to new yarn

Step 3 **Sew end of new warp yarn into weaving and wind around straight pin**

new warp yarn

inkle strap
shoelaces

YOUR PIPE LOOM IS READY AND WAITING for you to start with an interesting and easy technique called inkle weaving. Inkles are straps and inkle weaving is a way to weave strong and beautiful straps of any width. Inkle straps are warp-faced, which means you only see the warp in the finished piece and the weft (side to side yarn) only shows a little at the edges. In addition to shoelaces, you can use this technique to make headbands, belts, chokers, friendship bracelets, backpack straps, and anything else you can imagine.

materials

loom

PIPE LOOM (WARPED ACCORDING TO METHOD 1 ON PAGE 62)

yarn

WARP YARN: SIZE 3 PEARL COTTON— 1 (5-GRAM) SKEIN PER SHOELACE

WEFT YARN: SIZE 3 PEARL COTTON— 1 (5-GRAM) SKEIN PER SHOELACE

SHUTTLE

SCISSORS

CLOTH MEASURING TAPE OR A SHOELACE FROM A PAIR OF YOUR FAVORITE SHOES TO MEASURE AGAINST

YARN NEEDLE

loom set-up *(see page 67)*

TOTAL WARP ENDS: 10

SETT: AS CLOSE AS YOU CAN MAKE IT

WARP WIDTH: APPROXIMATELY 1" ON LOOM BEFORE WEAVING (AFTER YOU START WEAVING, THE WIDTH NAR- ROWS TO $1/4$")

HEDDLES: 5

finished size
$1/4$" wide and approximately 42" long

Mismatch Style
Who needs matching shoelaces?
Not you—when you weave your own.

selvedges

To help keep your edges (also known as selvedges) even as you weave, with one hand, hold some tension on the loop of weft at the edge as you gradually pull it through the warp with the other hand as shown below.

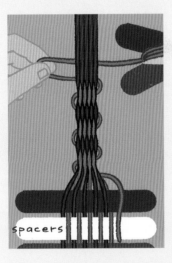

spacers

If while you're working, you see the weft showing between the warps, the warp might be too tight. Loosen it slightly by loosening the straps. It's just about right when, if you press down on the row you just completed extra-firmly with the shuttle, the whole warp will move down slightly.

1 prepare loom

Warp the loom following the instructions starting on page 62, making sure to follow the Loom Set-Up Specifications on page 74.

2 determine shoelace length

To figure out the correct length for your shoelaces, either measure a shoelace currently on the shoes for which you are making the laces or follow this guide: for shoes with 3 or 4 holes, make 27" laces; for shoes with 5 holes, make 36" laces; for shoes with 6 holes, make 40" laces; for shoes with 7 holes, make 45" laces.

3 start to weave

Wind your weft onto a shuttle (see page 71) and open one of the sheds (the space between the threads that are up and the threads that are down). To do this, move the shed stick up to the top of the loom or move it down and pull it toward the heddle bar. Pass the shuttle through the open shed, leaving a 5" tail sticking out the side where you began.

4 change shed and continue weaving

Change the shed so that the threads that were up in step 3 are down now and the ones that were down in step 3 are up now. Pass the shuttle back across the new open shed but—instead of going all the way across in one movement—stop in the middle and press firmly down on what you've just woven with the flat edge of your shuttle before continuing through. Pull the yarn tight when you get to the other side.

Change the shed so that the one that was open when you started is open again. Pass the weft back through this new open shed, once again using your shuttle to press down what you have woven when you are halfway through.

To pull warp threads close together to cover up weft (except at edges), grasp both ends of the weft (the loose tail end and the end of the yarn that is wrapped on the shuttle) and pull them firmly in opposite directions. Put down the tail end. Your weaving will now be about $\frac{1}{4}$" wide.

Continue weaving, being careful to keep your edges (selvedges) even by following the instructions at left.

Step 4 *Pass shuttle halfway through open shed and press down on previous row*

use shuttle to pack down yarn

spacers

Step 4 *Pull both ends of warp so weft threads "disappear"*

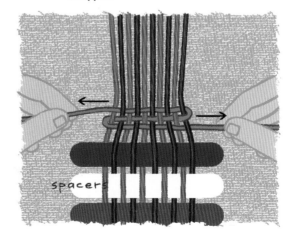

spacers

5 advance warp and continue weaving

Advance the warp when the shed gets small and there is not much space for your shuttle to pass through. Do this by slightly loosening the tension straps at the bottom of the loom and moving the woven shoelace down and around the cloth bar. If the tension is just right, you can also simply press down extra hard with the shuttle while you are weaving, moving the warp slightly with each row.

Weave until the shoelace is as long as you want it to be. Measure the shoelaces with a cloth measuring tape or with an existing shoelace that is the length that you want the lace on the loom to be.

6 finishing

To secure the ends of the shoelace, thread the weft tail that is sticking out at the beginning onto a yarn needle and sew it back and forth across the shoelace at least twice to make sure that it will not come out. Cut the weft tail close to where it comes out of the side of the weaving. Repeat at the other end.

Remove the shed stick, cut the shoelace off the loom by cutting the warp in the middle of the unwoven part and sliding the warp strands out of the heddles. Save the heddles for your next project. Remove the craft-stick spacers at the bottom of the loom.

Trim the excess warp still extending from the shoelace about $\frac{1}{2}$" from where you started weaving. To stiffen the ends of the shoelace so that you can put them into your shoe easily, tightly wrap a piece of tape about 2" long around them. Wrap it tightly and at an angle so that it ends up as a small point off the end of the lace. If desired, remove the tape after the lace is threaded onto your shoe.

striped shoelaces

For two-color striped shoelaces, change colors while warping your loom as follows: When you start your warp, wind 3 times around the top and cloth bars. Stop. At the cloth bar, firmly knot a second color onto the first color, then cut off the excess yarn of the first color. Wind 4 times around with the new color. Stop. At the cloth bar, firmly knot the original color to the second color (cutting off excess yarn of second color after it is tied) and wind the last 3 warp threads. End at the bottom by clipping the end of the yarn to the clothespin.

Getting Comfortable at Your Loom

THE PIPE LOOM IS A VERSATILE TOOL. THERE ARE A NUMBER OF WAYS TO SET IT UP BOTH FOR WARPING AND FOR WEAVING. HERE ARE A FEW WAYS TO USE IT. TRY SEVERAL SO THAT YOU CAN FIND A WAY TO WEAVE THAT IS THE MOST COMFORTABLE FOR YOU.

Sit on the floor with the loom standing on its legs in front of you.

Sit on the floor and lean the loom against a table or wall. Remove the T joints on the legs, turn them sideways and reattach the 8" sections so they point down toward the ground to make it taller.

Sit in a chair with the loom in your lap and the top propped against a table. You can remove the legs for this method.

Stand the loom on a low table and sit on a chair or stool in front of it.

Stand the loom on a higher table or counter, so you can stand in front of it.

tapestry
dog collar
and belt

TAPESTRY IS A CELEBRATION OF different colors next to each other, and it is the weaving technique that people all over the world use to tell their stories. In a tapestry, the weft (side to side yarn) does not go all the way from one edge to the other edge but instead is woven back and forth over a small section of warp. If you have been working on the projects in this book, you might already have done some tapestry—the blocks of color at the top of the Treasure Pouch on page 38 are basic tapestry shapes. You can use the same technique to make a great collar for a special dog, a unique belt for yourself, or even a matching set for the two of you.

finished size

dog collar: $1^1/_2$" wide and about 6" longer than generous neck measurement of dog for whom collar is being made

belt: 1" wide and 6" to 8" longer than generous waist/hip measurement of person for whom belt is being made

materials

loom

PIPE LOOM (warped according to Method 1 on page 62)

yarn

WARP YARN: 30 YARDS 100% WOOL NAVAJO WARP FOR DOG COLLAR OR 20 YARDS FOR BELT (see Sources for Supplies)

WEFT YARN: 8 (5-GRAM) SKEINS PATERNAYAN TAPESTRY YARN (2 SKEINS EACH OF 4 DIFFERENT COLORS) FOR DOG COLLAR OR BELT

SCISSORS

FORK

SHARP YARN NEEDLE

$1^1/_2$" SIDE-RELEASE PLASTIC BUCKLE AND GLIDE FOR DOG COLLAR OR 1" BUCKLE FOR BELT (available at fabric and camping supply stores)

loom set-up (see page 67)

TOTAL WARP ENDS: 16 FOR DOG COLLAR; 10 FOR BELT

SETT: 8 E.P.I. FOR BOTH DOG COLLAR AND BELT

WARP WIDTH ON LOOM: 2" FOR DOG COLLAR; $1^1/_4$" FOR BELT

HEDDLES: 8 FOR DOG COLLAR; 5 FOR BELT

1 determine length

To determine the length for the dog collar, measure the dog's neck with a measuring tape, then add 6" to that measurement. For the belt, measure the waist or hips of the person who will wear the belt (depending on where that person wants to wear it), then add 6" to 8".

2 prepare loom

Warp the loom following the instructions on page 62, making sure to follow the Loom Set-Up Specifications for either the dog collar or belt on page 80. Twine across the warp as explained at right.

3 prepare weft yarn

Pull out and cut a length of weft yarn about 12" long. Paternayan Tapestry Yarn comes with 3 strands lightly twisted together. Divide the length of yarn by separating 2 of the strands from the third. You can weave with 2 strands or with the single strand. Try both and see which you like better. Two strands goes faster but one strand makes more delicate shapes. Because you are using short lengths of yarn, you will not need to wind the yarn onto a shuttle.

4 weave one shape

Open one shed and weave halfway across (8 warp ends for the dog collar, 5 ends for the belt), pulling the tail of the weft yarn until the end is just inside the edge of the warp.

Change the shed and beat (press the weft down with your fork, see page 41). Tapestries are called weft-faced weavings, which means that the colored weft completely covers the warp. The fork is used to press each row of weft, gently but firmly, onto the row before.

Bring the weft back across the area you just wove, bubbling well. If you don't bubble well, your weaving will pull in at the edges. Change the shed and beat.

twining

Twining is a technique used to keep the warp threads a certain distance apart and to establish the width of the weaving. To twine, you twist 2 strands of yarn alternately around warp threads, as follows.

1 Cut a piece of warp yarn about 48" long (this is the length of yarn needed for the pipe loom used in this book; if you weave on a wider loom, you'll need a longer piece of yarn). Fold it in half and make a loop knot around the left side bar (see page 31, which shows the loop knot made around a pencil). Knot the 2 ends right next to the left side of the warp.

2 Twine by alternately putting each strand behind a warp thread and pulling it out again to the front. Pull each strand tightly as you twine.

3 At the right side, tie a knot right next to the edge warp. This keeps the edge warp from shifting out of position. Tie or tape the ends of the twining yarn to the right side bar.

When you advance the warp, be sure to cut the ends of the twining yarn where they are attached to the side bars.

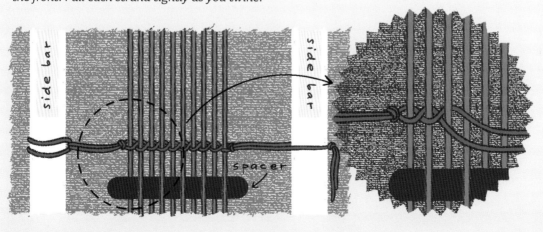

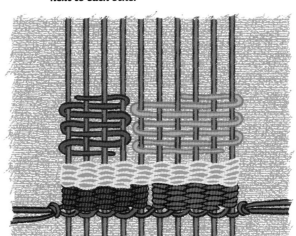

Continue to weave back and forth over the same section of warp until your piece of weft is used up or you have woven a square or rectangle that is as tall as you want it to be but not taller than 1" for this project. Remember to bubble well and to change the shed before you beat.

Weave another square or rectangle next to the first with a new color (see illustration above).

Notice the gap between the two squares that you have woven. This is called a "slit" and this technique is called slit tapestry.

5 continue weaving

After finishing the first 2 shapes, weave with another color from edge to edge, then make more squares or rectangles with the slit in a different place than the first one. Try different color and shape combinations as you go or make a repeating pattern.

Weave until your dog collar or belt is the length desired.

6 *finishing*

Twine across again at the end of your weaving to keep that end from unraveling. Cut your weaving off the loom by cutting the warp threads below the craft sticks that are your spacers, saving the heddles for another project.

Wash and full your dog collar or belt (see page 109). Trim any bits of weft that stick out where you started and stopped new pieces of yarn, cutting them close to the weaving.

On the end that will be sewn around the buckle, trim the fringe to about $\frac{1}{2}$" from the twining. On the other end, leave a few inches of fringe. Wrap the trimmed end around one side of the buckle and sew it in place with a strand of weft yarn threaded on a sharp yarn needle. Feed the fringed end through the glide, around the other side of the buckle and back through the glide. This allows you to adjust the size to fit your dog's neck or your waist or hips!

Bryn and Willow enjoy each other—and their matching accessories.

Weaving Around the World

ALMOST EVERY COUNTRY HAS A WEAVING TRADITION. MANY DEVELOPED BASED ON THE RESOURCES WEAVERS HAD AVAILABLE TO THEM A LONG TIME AGO. FOR EXAMPLE, THE YARNS USED WERE ORIGINALLY DETERMINED BY THE TYPES OF FIBER-PRODUCING ANIMALS AND PLANTS THAT LIVED IN EACH AREA AND THE COLORS THAT COULD BE EXTRACTED FROM NATIVE PLANTS AND INSECTS.

The **Navajo** people in the **southwestern United States** are known for weaving beautiful wool rugs, blankets, and tapestries. Traditionally, these rugs feature symbolic geometric shapes.

In **Central Asia**, carpet weaving has been part of nomadic life for centuries. Multicolored flat carpets called kilims and fluffy pile carpets are used to sit on and are sewn into bags and saddle blankets for camels.

France and **Belgium** are known for the weaving of intricate pictorial tapestries, often including flowers, animals, and stories depicting royal life or stories from the Bible or ancient mythology.

Handwoven woolen sails made it possible for Christopher Columbus to sail to the **New World** and for **Viking** explorers to sail throughout **Europe** and to **North America.** Today sails are made with synthetic materials, but modern weavers weave woolen sails for historical reenactments.

Scandinavia is well known for its many weaving traditions. Especially popular are linen items for the home, such as napkins, place mats, and hand towels, and rugs woven from scrap fabric (called rag rugs).

In **Scotland**, people have been weaving a checked cloth called tartan for hundreds of years. Different patterns are thought to represent different regions or clans (families).

In **Guatemala**, weavers create complex, brightly-colored blankets and clothing, including shirts called *huipiles* (pronounced whee peels), belts they sometimes wrap around their heads like turbans, and skirts.

In **New Zealand**, the **Maori** people use fiber from native flax plants to weave many items, including baskets, floor mats, and cloaks.

New Zealand

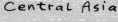
Central Asia

France and Belgium

International Explorations

Scandinavia

North America

Scotland

Guatemala

advancing on a
pipe loom

People say that the best designs never go out of fashion.
In the case of the pipe loom, this is certainly true. While it is made from
modern plumbing parts, its design dates back to the ancient Babylonians.
It has probably endured for so long because it can be used for
so many different weaving techniques.

This chapter introduces a new way to warp your pipe loom so that
you can make a scarf, a small carpet, and even a blanket. The main difference
between Warping Method 1 (which you learned in the previous chapter) and
Warping Method 2 (introduced here) is the pattern you follow
when winding the warp on the loom.

warping a pipe loom—method 2

THIS WARPING METHOD CAN BE USED FOR EVERYTHING, FROM NARROW BANDS TO PIECES THE FULL WIDTH OF YOUR LOOM (HOWEVER, METHOD 1 ON PAGE 62 IS GENERALLY EASIER FOR BANDS LESS THAN 2" WIDE AND FOR INKLE BANDS REGARDLESS OF WIDTH). FOR MOST WEAVING IT IS IMPORTANT TO KEEP THE STRANDS OF WARP SEPARATED FROM EACH OTHER AND THIS WARPING METHOD DOES THIS BETTER THAN WARPING METHOD 1 ON PAGE 62.

materials

SAME MATERIALS AS FOR METHOD 1 (*see page 62*)

PLUS 2 ADDITIONAL PIECES OF DOWEL (THE 13" CLOTH BAR AND THE 11" BIG SHED STICK)

1   prepare warp and heddle bar

Put a piece of tape all the way across the front of the warp bar (the 13" piece of dowel) and mark it as you did with the top bar and the cloth bar (see page 62).

If the heddle bar is in the heddle bar frame, take it out.

2   position and tension cloth bar

Adjust the tension straps and tape the cloth bar to the side bars (see page 63), leaving 3" to 4" between the bottom frame bar and the cloth bar. Attach a clothespin or strong clip to one of the straps at the bottom, so you can stop while warping (if necessary) and not lose tension.

3   position warp bar

Put the warp bar (13" dowel) into the elbows of the heddle bar frame (this is temporary). You may have to push the elbows slightly inward so the warp bar can rest in them. Make sure the inch marks on the warp bar are visible. Tape the ends of the warp bar to the elbows so it can't slide out.

Step 4 *Tie beginning of warp to warp bar*

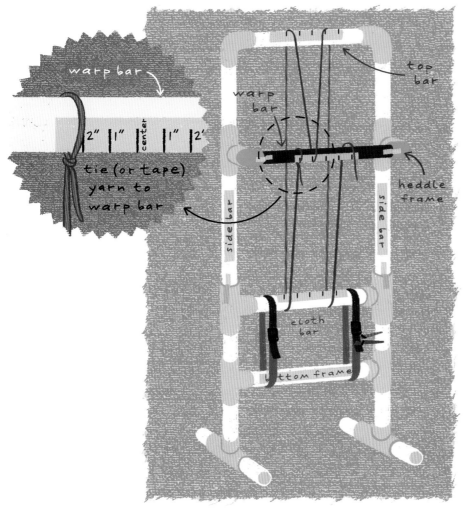

warp bar

2" 1" center 1" 2"

tie (or tape) yarn to warp bar

warp bar

top bar

heddle frame

side bar

side bar

cloth bar

bottom frame

Step 5 **Wind warp**

- Beginning at the warp bar, bring the warp yarn down and under the cloth bar (front to back)

- All the way up the back and over the top bar (back to front)

- Down and under the warp bar (back to front, reversing direction)

- Back up and over the top bar (front to back)

- Down the back and under the cloth bar (back to front)

- Up and over the warp bar (back to front reversing direction again)

- Down to the cloth bar

Repeat until you have the number of warp ends specified in your project. Clip the end of the warp yarn securely with the clothespin so the warp won't unwind.

Tip!
It's important to always wind from back to front when reversing direction at the warp bar. Check your work frequently to make sure the pattern is correct.

4   attach warp to warp bar

Wind your warp yarn into a ball that you can hold in your hand so that it will unwind easily. Look at the instructions for your project and note the width of the warp.

Secure the beginning of your warp to the warp bar by tying it to the warp bar in a tight knot or by winding it at least three times around the warp bar and taping it securely. Attach it to the left of the center mark, half of the width of your warp. If your warp is 4" wide, you will attach your warp 2" to the left of center.

5   wind warp

There is a very particular pattern for winding on the warp. Look at the illustration on page 91 and follow the instructions given there. You will be making a continuous loop around the cloth bar and top bar, but instead of going around and around in the same direction as you did in Method 1, you will reverse direction at the warp bar each time you come to it. Try to keep the tension on the warp firm and even as you wind. Check your work frequently.

6   check warp

Adjust the tension on the warp so that it is even; if necessary, take up any slack on individual threads by pulling them tighter, one by one, and then repositioning the clothespin (this tightening process is similar to the way you tighten shoelaces one by one until you get to the point where the laces are no longer traveling through the holes and then all the extra slack is pulled out). The warp should feel tight like a trampoline, not floppy.

Adjust the warp threads on all 3 bars so that the warp is the correct width and the threads are evenly spaced. The instructions for each project will tell you both the correct width for the project and how far apart the warp threads should be from each other (how far apart the warp threads are from each other is called the sett; see page 67).

7   secure warp

Wrap the end of the yarn at least 3 times around the warp bar on the right, the same distance from the center as you started on the left. Tie or tape it securely to the bar. Cut off extra warp yarn.

Warping method 2—Steps 1–7 (completed)

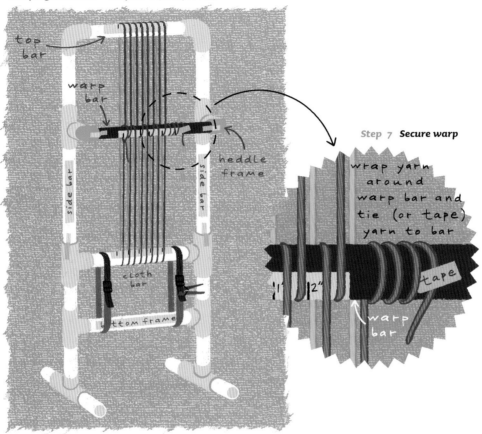

top bar

warp bar

side bar

side bar

heddle frame

cloth bar

bottom frame

Step 7 **Secure warp**

wrap yarn around warp bar and tie (or tape) yarn to bar

1"

2"

tape

warp bar

8 position warp

Remove the tape holding together the warp bar and heddle frame. Remove warp bar from heddle frame elbows by jiggling it out and sliding it slightly sideways. Notice how you can make the entire loop of warp rotate by moving the warp bar. Move the warp bar down until it is a couple of inches above the cloth bar. Remove the tape from the cloth bar where it is attached to the side bars and tighten the tension straps: Your warp should feel tight like a trampoline and the warp bar should be hard to move up and down.

9 prepare sheds and heddles and install big shed stick

Make the sheds (see page 65) and the heddles (see page 66). Install the heddles (see page 66).

Turn the top craft stick on its side to open the shed and slide the 11" length of dowel (the big shed stick) into this space. Remove the craft stick from the loom. You will use the big shed stick to open and close the sheds by sliding it up to the top of the loom or down to the heddles. Open the shed by sliding the big shed stick down to press firmly against the heddles.

10 open and close sheds and weave in spacers

Practice opening and closing the sheds by pushing the shed stick up and then pulling it down. If the shed is hard to open, there are 3 remedies to try: strum the warp threads with your fingers as though you are playing the guitar, adjust the tension by tightening or loosening the straps (it could be too tight OR too loose), or find a dowel with a larger diameter to use as a shed stick.

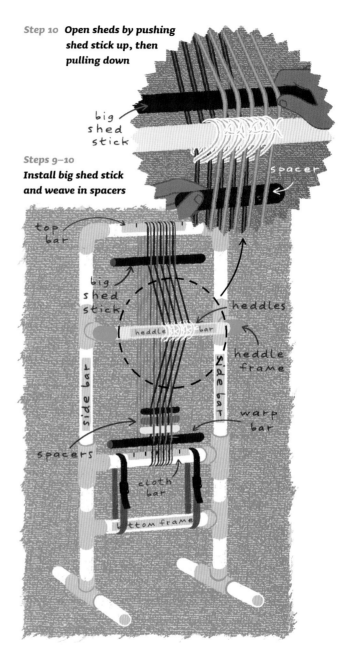

Step 10 **Open sheds by pushing shed stick up, then pulling down**

big shed stick

spacer

Steps 9–10
Install big shed stick and weave in spacers

top bar

big shed stick

heddles

heddle bar

heddle frame

side bar

side bar

warp bar

spacers

cloth bar

bottom frame

Weave in 3 or 4 spacers (see page 69). You are now ready to weave.

advancing warp

When you have woven enough that your sheds are getting small and it's hard to pass the shuttle through, advance the warp to create more weaving room, as follows.

1 Bring your big shed stick down so that it rests gently against the heddles—this will help to keep it from falling out when you release the tension. Then gently loosen the tension on the straps until the warp is saggy and push the straps toward the side bars.

2 Grasp the warp bar with both hands and gently push it down, under, and around the cloth bar, carefully maneuvering the warp bar between the tension straps and always leaving about 3" woven cloth above the cloth bar.

3 Check that your weaving is straight, then tighten the straps again, making sure that the warp is tight and the shed

stick stays at the top of the loom when you push it up there. The heddles may have angled downward. Push them back up until they are again pointing straight toward the heddle bar.

weaving
bag *with*
inkle strap

THIS RECTANGULAR BAG IS GOOD FOR
holding weaving supplies, such as shuttles
and heddles. It is made from two separately
woven parts, each of which uses a different
warping and weaving technique. The strap
uses warping method 1 and is a warp-faced
inkle band just like the shoelaces on page
74. This means that the warp, the up and
down yarn, is spaced very closely together
so that you do not see any weft, the side-to-
side yarn. The body of the bag uses warping
method 2. It is weft-faced, which means
that each row of weft is pressed down firmly
so that it completely covers the warp.

finished size

strap: 1" × 45"

bag (before sewing together): 3 ³/₄" × 24"

materials

loom

strap: PIPE LOOM WARPED USING
METHOD 1 (SEE PAGE 62) WITH
3 COLORS AS FOLLOWS: 6 STRANDS
COLOR #1, 3 STRANDS COLOR #2,
2 STRANDS COLOR #3, 3 STRANDS
COLOR #2, 6 STRANDS COLOR #1.
(*Change colors by tying new color
to previous color at cloth bar as for
striped shoelaces on page 78.*)

bag: PIPE LOOM WARPED USING
METHOD 2 (*see page 90*)

warp yarn

strap: APPROXIMATELY 12 YARDS EACH
OF 3 COLORS OF STRONG RUG WOOL,
SUCH AS KLIPPEN ASBORYA (*see
Sources for Supplies*)

bag: 40 YARDS STRONG COTTON STRING
OR 12/12 SEINE TWINE (*see Sources
for Supplies*)

weft yarn

strap: 8 ADDITIONAL YARDS SAME
STRONG RUG WOOL USED FOR WARP,
IN ONE OF COLORS USED FOR WARP

bag: 125 YARDS STRONG RUG WOOL,
SUCH AS KLIPPEN ASBORYA OR
BROWN SHEEP LAMB'S PRIDE BULKY,
IN COLORS TO MATCH STRAP (*see
Sources for Supplies*)

SCISSORS

SHUTTLE

FORK

YARN NEEDLE

Sizing Up!
If you want your bag
to be wider, keep the sett (see
page 67) the same but add more
warp ends at the edges. If you
want it longer, weave extra rows.

TOTAL WARP ENDS: 20 FOR STRAP
    AND BAG

sett

strap: AS CLOSE AS YOU CAN MAKE IT

bag: 5 E.P.I.

warp width on loom

strap: APPROXIMATELY 2" ON THE LOOM
    BEFORE WEAVING (AFTER YOU START
    WEAVING, THE WIDTH NARROWS TO
    APPROXIMATELY 1")

bag: 4"

HEDDLES: 10 FOR STRAP AND BAG

1   weave strap

Warp the loom following the instructions on page 62, making sure to follow the Loom Set-Up specifications above and the color sequence given in materials list on page 96.

Wind your shuttle with weft yarn (see page 71). Weave the strap following the instructions for the shoelaces on page 74. Note that this warp will be sticky because the yarn is fuzzy. You may need to put your fingers into the warp to open the shed (the space between the threads that are up and the threads that are down) before weaving

across and using your shuttle to beat each strand of weft into place.

Leave long fringe on both ends when you cut the strap off of the loom.

2   get ready to weave bag

Warp the loom following the instructions on page 90, making sure to follow the Loom Set-Up specifications at left.

Using a piece of cotton warp yarn, twine across the warp to space it and keep it from unraveling after you have finished the body of the bag (see page 83). Remember to tie knots at each side of the warp and to cut twining yarn where it attaches to the side bars when you advance the warp.

3   start weaving bag

Wind a shuttle with weft yarn (see page 71) and open one shed if one isn't already open (see page 68). Starting at one side of the loom front, pass the shuttle full of yarn through the shed across to the other side. Gently pull the yarn so the tail (cut end) is just inside the edge of the warp and is

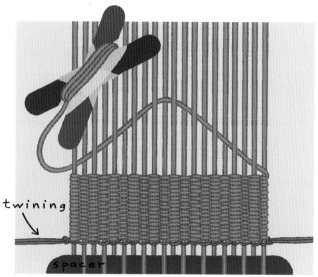

twining

spacer

tucked under the first warp thread. Open the other shed and pass the shuttle in the opposite direction through this shed the same way that you did on the first row, bubbling well.

Open the other shed and use a fork (beater) to push the bubbled weft to the bottom of the loom so that it is flat (this is called beating). For more on bubbling and beating, see page 41. For this project, you want to be sure that the warp threads stay the correct distance apart from each other so that the weft yarn will pack down to completely cover the warp (bubbling and beating well make this possible).

Continue to weave back and forth, bubbling and beating, advancing the warp when necessary (see page 95), and changing colors for stripes (see page 43) whenever you like until the piece is about 20" to 24" long.

Check your width regularly to make sure the edges are not pulling in. Remember that you want a lot of weft in each row and that the "extra" yarn formed by the bubble should be in the middle of the weaving, not sticking out as a loop at the edge. If it starts to get narrow, make your bubbles bigger in the middle (more weft in the middle of each row pushes the warp threads apart).

4 remove weaving from loom

Using a piece of warp yarn, twine across the top of the weaving to hold it in place, remembering to tie knots at each side of the warp (see page 83). Remove the big shed stick by pulling it out of the warp, cut the warp off at the warp bar, and remove your weaving from the loom, saving the heddles for another project.

Take out the spacers and knot adjacent pairs of warp threads together on both ends of the weaving. You will have a fringe at both ends.

5 assemble bag

Full the bag and strap according to the instructions on page 109.

When dry, fold the bag in half lengthwise and find the center. This will be the bottom of your bag. Thread a tapestry needle with a 40" length of yarn the same color as the edge warps of the strap. Pull the yarn through the bag at the center of the bottom on one side (as shown in the illustration at right). Leave half of it hanging out to sew up the second side.

Sew the bottom and one side of the strap to one side of the bag. When you are about 2½" from the top, sew around 2 or 3 times in the same place to make a strong edge and then bury the end of the yarn by passing the needle through the fabric you've woven. Cut the yarn close to where it sticks out of the weaving. With the other end of yarn still sticking out at the bottom of the bag, sew the strap in so that one side of the bag is now closed. Repeat with another 40" length of yarn on the other side of the bag. Trim fringe on both flaps and knot or braid fringe on both sides of strap, if desired.

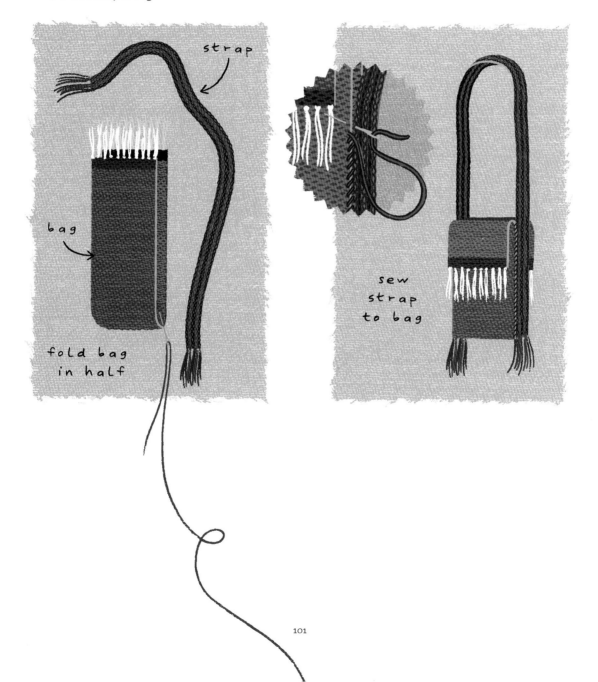

strap

bag

fold bag
in half

sew
strap
to bag

chenille scarf

WHAT COULD BE COZIER THAN WRAPPING yourself in a soft cotton scarf that drapes around your neck and tickles your chin? Making your scarf soft rather than firm, however, requires something called a balanced weave. This means that the warp (the up and down yarn) and the weft (the side to side yarn) both show. Most fabric for clothing is woven in a balanced weave. Other projects in this book have been warp-faced, which means that only the warp shows, and weft-faced, which means that only the weft shows. These techniques make fabric that is strong and often stiff—perfect for a rug or a shoelace but not a snugly scarf.

1 get ready

Warp the loom following the instructions on page 90, making sure to follow the Loom Set-Up specifications at right.

materials

PIPE LOOM WARPED ACCORDING TO METHOD 2 ON PAGE 90

WARP AND WEFT YARN: 1 (50-GRAM; 98-YARD) SKEIN CRYSTAL PALACE COTTON CHENILLE (*see Sources for Supplies*)

ABOUT 28" LONG PIECE SCRAP YARN OR CLOTH STRIP, FOR HEADER

SCISSORS

SHUTTLE

FORK

loom set-up (see page 67)

TOTAL WARP ENDS: 30

SETT: 10 E.P.I.

WARP WIDTH ON LOOM: APPROXIMATELY 3" ON THE LOOM BEFORE WEAVING (*after you start weaving, the width narrows to about* $2\frac{3}{4}$")

HEDDLES: 15

finished size

$2\frac{3}{4}$" x 43"

2 weave header

A header is a short section of weaving that helps to space the warp before starting the actual piece. This section of weaving will come out when you are finished with your scarf.

Using the piece of scrap yarn or cloth strip, weave 3 rows above the spacers, following step 3 of the instructions for the Weaving Bag on page 98 except beat gently after each row and leave both ends of your scrap yarn hanging out the sides.

3 weave scarf

Wind a shuttle with weft yarn (see page 71) and open one shed if one is not already open. Starting at one side of the loom front, pass the shuttle full of yarn through the open shed across to the other side. Gently pull the yarn so the tail (cut end) sticks out of the edge of the warp about 2".

Open the other shed and, with your fingers, tuck the 2" tail into the new shed. Pass the shuttle in the opposite direction through this shed the same way that you did on the first row, bubbling well (see page 41).

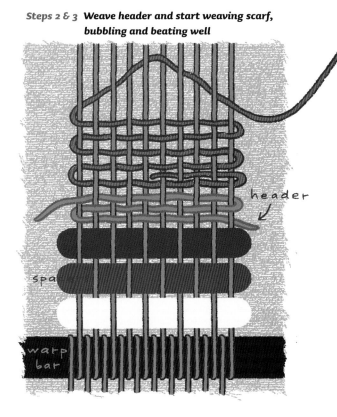

Steps 2 & 3 *Weave header and start weaving scarf, bubbling and beating well*

Open the other shed and use a fork (beater) to very gently push the bubbled weft to the bottom of the loom so that it is flat but there is still space between the weft rows. For this project, and most balanced weaves, you want to be sure that the rows of weft stay about the same distance apart as the strands of warp: ideally, there will be tiny squares of empty space (and a little chenille fuzz) between the strands of warp and the strands of weft.

Continue to weave back and forth, advancing the warp (see page 95) and adding new yarn when necessary (see page 43). If you are weaving carefully and bubbling well, your weaving will stay approximately the correct width, although you will probably notice a little draw-in (see right). If your weaving isn't the correct width, see page 117 to learn about unweaving. Weave until the scarf goes all the way up the back of the loom, the warp bar has come over the top bar, and it is hard to make a shed through which you can fit your shuttle. Your scarf should be 40" to 45" long.

4 *finishing*

Remove the big shed stick and cut the warp threads at the warp bar. Remove the scarf from the loom, saving the heddles for another project. Take out the spacers if they haven't fallen out.

At the end where you finished weaving, knot pairs of adjacent warp threads together firmly against the fabric. Take out the header at the other end of scarf and knot pairs of adjacent warp threads together at this end too. If desired, make twisted fringe with groups of 4 warp threads (see page 45). Wash scarf gently (see page 109) and lay flat to dry.

draw-in

If there is not enough weft in each row, your project can get narrower as you weave. This is called draw-in and it is particularly noticeable when you are weaving back and forth in a balanced weave. There is always a little draw in for the first $1/4$" to $1/2$" when you begin to weave. But after that the width of the weaving should stay the same. To keep your weaving the same width, bubble well and make sure that the extra weft (meaning the extra yarn used in the bubble) is in the middle of the scarf, not at the edge.

At first you will have to think about evenly spacing every row of weft that goes across but soon your hands will know what to do automatically and you will get better at keeping the edges even. Keeping edges straight is something weavers work at all of their lives.

west african
blanket

IF YOU EVER LOOK CLOSELY AT A spiderweb, you will see that it is actually woven, which is why the world is full of myths linking weaving and spiders. According to one West African myth, the spider Anansi, a trickster as well as a source of great wisdom, taught the men of West Africa to weave kente cloth. Kente cloth is a fabric made of long narrow strips of woven cloth that have been sewn together.

Your pipe loom is not designed to weave very wide pieces of cloth, so like the weavers of West Africa, you will need to follow Anansi's advice and weave strips to create this blanket.

finished size

Each piece will be 2$\frac{1}{2}$", 3$\frac{1}{2}$", 4$\frac{1}{2}$", or 5" wide by 42" long. The finished blanket will be approximately 30" × 42" before washing and fulling. After washing, the blanket will be approximately 26" wide by 36" long, not counting the fringe. You can weave each section a different width but, because you are using the same yarn for each strip, the sett has to stay the same.

materials

PIPE LOOM WARPED USING METHOD 2 (SEE PAGE 90)

WARP AND WEFT YARN: 5 TO 7 (100-GRAM; 200-YARD SKEINS) HARRISVILLE HIGHLAND STYLE WOOL, EACH A DIFFERENT COLOR (*see Sources for Supplies*); EACH SKEIN WILL MAKE ONE 4$\frac{1}{2}$" OR 5" STRIP AND ONE 2$\frac{1}{2}$" STRIP, OR TWO 3$\frac{1}{2}$" STRIPS

APROXIMATELY 28"-LONG PIECE SCRAP YARN OR CLOTH STRIP, FOR HEADER

SCISSORS

SHUTTLE

FORK

YARN NEEDLE

loom set-up (see page 67)

TOTAL WARP ENDS: 24, 34, 44, OR 50

SETT: 10 E.P.I.

WARP WIDTH ON LOOM: 2$\frac{1}{2}$, 3$\frac{1}{2}$, 4$\frac{1}{2}$, OR 5"

HEDDLES: 12, 17, 22, OR 25

Teamwork!
**This blanket makes a great fundraiser.
Ask each participant to weave a strip,
then assemble and raffle it off to raise
funds for endangered animals, a group
trip, or more weaving yarn!**

1   *get ready*

Warp the loom following the instructions on page 90, making sure to follow the Loom Set-Up specifications on page 106.

2   *weave*

To make a blanket like the one shown in the photograph, weave 9 strips in the following widths:

    1 strip: 5" wide
    2 strips: $4\frac{1}{2}$" wide
    2 strips: $3\frac{1}{2}$" wide
    4 strips: $2\frac{1}{2}$" wide

To do this, follow the instructions for the Chenille Scarf on page 104 for each one.

3   *finishing*

After all the strips are woven, arrange them on a flat surface in a color pattern you like. Using leftover yarn threaded on a yarn needle, sew them together so the strips are butted up against each other as shown in the illustration below.

Finish edges with twisted fringe following the instructions on page 45.

Wash and full the blanket following the instructions at right.

Step 3 *Sew together strips to create blanket*

washing & fulling

It's often a good idea to wash a wool weaving when you take it off the loom to relax and soften the yarn. Many wool weavings also need to be fulled. Fulling is a process of gently agitating a weaving when it is wet so that the individual fibers of which the yarn is made start tangling around each other and turning into felt. The more you rub, scrub, and roll the wool while it is wet, the tighter the strands will hold on. Fulling makes a weaving softer, stronger, and more water-resistant.

On the Outer Hebrides, islands off the northwest coast of Scotland, handweavers make very special wool fabric called Harris Tweed that is famous around the world for its strength, warmth, and beauty. Fulling each piece of cloth is part of what makes it so wonderful, as is the singing of special fulling songs, which make the work of fulling more enjoyable. See if you can make up a chant that fits your rubbing rhythm as you full your woolen projects.

1 Fill a small tub with warm to hot water and a dash of liquid detergent or dish soap. Immerse your weaving in the water and let it soak for about 10 minutes.

2 If you want to full your weaving, "work" the piece by squeezing it, rubbing it, folding it, and swishing it around in the water for a few minutes. If you only want to wash your weaving, skip this step. When ready, squeeze the water out of the weaving and then remove it from the tub.

3 Refill the tub with fresh warm to hot water and put the piece back in. If you are fulling, rub and rinse it at the same time. If you are only washing, squeeze the weaving gently to remove the soapy water; do not rub it. Repeat this step with fresh water until all of the soap is removed from the weaving.

4 Squeeze the water out of the weaving and transfer it from the tub to a dry, clean towel. Roll the weaving in the towel to remove more water, then lay it flat on a second clean, dry towel to dry.

magic carpet *coasters* & *rugs*

WOULDN'T IT BE WONDERFUL TO BE able to fly on a carpet! Although it is probably only possible in our imaginations, these magic carpets, called pile carpets, are still fun to weave and to use in a dollhouse or as coasters (or for whatever other kind of fun you can dream up). They are made of short pieces of different-colored yarn knotted around pairs of warp threads to create special multicolored designs. People in Middle Eastern countries, such as Turkey, Iran, and Kazakhstan, have been using this technique to make rugs for thousands of years.

materials

PIPE LOOM WARPED USING METHOD 2 (*see page 90*)

WARP YARN: APPROXIMATELY 100 YARDS STRONG, FINE WOOL WARP YARN, SUCH AS BROWN SHEEP COMPANY NAVAJO 100% WOOL WARP, OR A STRONG COTTON STRING OR 12/12 SEINE TWINE (*see Sources for Supplies*); ENOUGH FOR 3 CARPETS

WEFT YARN: 6 (5-GRAM) SKEINS PATERNAYAN TAPESTRY YARN, IN 6 DIFFERENT COLORS (ENOUGH FOR 1 CARPET)

25 YARDS MORE WARP YARN FOR CONTINUOUS WEFT AND PROTECTIVE EDGES

2 SHUTTLES

LARGE, SHARP SCISSORS

SMALL SCISSORS OR THREAD SNIPS

loom set-up (*see page 67*)

TOTAL WARP ENDS: 52

SETT: 12 E.P.I.

WARP WIDTH ON LOOM: $4\frac{1}{3}$"

HEDDLES: 26

finished size
Approximately 4" × 5"

1   getting ready

Carpet-making combines several techniques that are used elsewhere in this book so, while the carpets look really different, there is almost nothing new except the way that the techniques are combined. The knots are made just like the hair on the Rag Doll Warriors on page 46. After each row of different-colored knots, a length of fine yarn on a shuttle is woven from one side of the loom to the other and back again, just like weaving a scarf or a blanket. Called the continuous weft, these rows of back and forth weaving hold the knots in place.

Once your loom is warped for this project, you can weave up to 3 carpets in a row (without rewarping the loom).

2   prepare loom and graph

Warp the loom following the instructions on page 90, making sure to follow the Loom Set-Up specifications on page 110. Choose a graph to follow from the choices on page 119 or make your own.

Photocopy the graph and tape to side bars of loom, if desired. If you didn't learn to make Ghiordes knots to make the hair on the Rag Doll Warrior, then photocopy the knot instructions on page 50 so that you can refer to them easily (without flipping pages back and forth) while beginning this project.

3   space warp

Using warp yarn, twine to secure the edges (see page 83). Remember to tie knots at each side of the warp and to cut the twining yarn where it attaches to the side bars when you advance the warp (see page 95).

4   work bottom edge of carpet

Wind 2 to 3 yards of warp yarn onto a shuttle (see page 71). To protect the carpet's bottom edge from wear and tear, weave 5 rows above the twining following step 3 of Weaving the Bag on page 98. Remember to bubble well before you beat each row into place.

Step 5 *Weave carpet body in 4 steps (A–D)*

A *Work protective edges on both sides*

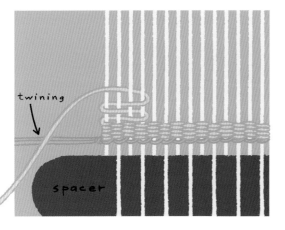

B *Make row of Ghiordes knots between protected side edges*

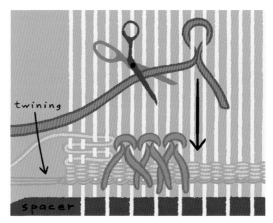

5   weave carpet body

To weave carpet body, repeat steps A–D in order for each row of graph.

A   Protect Side Edges of Weaving: Weave 3 rows protective edging (see right).

B   Make Ghiordes Knots: Following the instructions on page 50 but working directly from the skein of Paternayan yarn and using your fingers instead of a needle to manipulate the yarn around the warp threads, make Ghiordes knots with each color as it appears on the graph. Work all of the knots in one color in the same row at the same time if that seems easiest. Once you complete each knot, cut the yarn from the skein so that you have a tail of about $\frac{1}{2}$".

C   Work 2 Rows Plain Weaving: To hold the rows of individual knots and the wrapped edges together, using one of the shuttles full of yarn at a side edge, weave 2 rows all the way across and back—from one side of the loom to the other (covering the wrapped edges on both sides and the Ghiordes knots)—bubbling and beating well

C & D *Work 2 rows plain weaving (continuous weft) and trim knots*

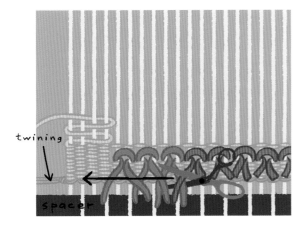

twining

spacer

after each row (see page 41). These rows are called the continuous weft.

D   Trim Knots: When your row of knots is secured in place with the 2 rows continuous weft, trim all of the knots in that row so that they are even, as follows: With large scissors held parallel to the weft, trim all of the yarn sticking out (called the pile) so that it is about the same length and sticks out $\frac{1}{4}$" to $\frac{3}{8}$" from the warp. Be careful not to cut the warp threads.

protecting side edges

To protect the right and left side edges of the carpet (in this case, the 4 warp threads at each side of the loom), you work the same "over, under" pattern of other weaving, but you treat 2 warp threads (a pair) as one. Read the directions below and refer to Illustration A at left.

First side: *Using a shuttle full of warp yarn on one side of your loom, take the yarn around the outside edge of the last warp thread, then behind the loom and up to the front in between the 2nd and 3rd warp threads, then return to the back of the loom by taking the yarn between the 4th and 5th warp threads, then come back to the front between the 2nd and 3rd warp threads. Repeat on the same warp threads until you have completed 3 rows. Drop shuttle and let hang from the weaving.*

Second side: *To protect the other side edge of the carpet, using a separate shuttle wound with 2 to 3 yards weft yarn, weave 3 rows using the same method used for the first side. Drop shuttle and let it hang from the weaving. (Note: The first time you do this, tuck the tail of weft yarn into the open shed.)*

6 weave top of carpet

When you have finished your graphed pattern, cut off the extra yarn used for protective edging at one edge and tuck the tail end into the weaving.

With the shuttle at the other edge, weave 5 rows continuous weft with warp yarn for the top edging, bubbling well. Cut the end, leaving a 2" tail and tuck it into the weaving.

Twine across as at the beginning of the carpet to hold everything in place. If you only want to weave one carpet, skip to step 8.

7 weave more carpets on same warp

If you want to weave another carpet, advance the warp (see page 95) until your finished carpet is on the back of the loom and there is 8" to 10" of warp in between (enough warp for several inches of fringe for both carpets).

Transfer the 3 spacers currently at the bottom of the first carpet to the space where you are going to weave your next carpet. Weave another carpet, starting with step 3 on page 113.

8 finishing

When you are finished weaving carpets, cut the warp at the warp bar and remove the carpets from your loom, saving the heddles for another project. Remove the spacers and cut carpets apart so there is an equal amount of fringe for each one. Wash and full your carpets (see page 109) and lay them flat to dry.

When a carpet is dry, if necessary, trim the pile to make it even and smooth. To make this easy, bend the carpet over something hard and curved like a soda bottle, so 1 or 2 rows at a time stick up and you can see exactly what you are doing. Be careful not to cut the pile too short! Brush off any loose ends and see if your carpet will fly.

Unweaving: The Story of Penelope

UNWEAVING CAN BE WONDERFUL. REALLY!
SOMETIMES, IF THINGS DO NOT LOOK THE WAY THAT YOU WANT THEM TO,
IT FEELS REALLY GOOD TO TAKE OUT SOME OF YOUR WORK AND REDO IT;
AT OTHER TIMES IT'S NOT WORTH IT. NO MATTER HOW CAREFUL YOU ARE THOUGH,
UNWEAVING WILL PROBABLY BE A PART OF YOUR WEAVING LIFE AND YOU
MIGHT AS WELL TRY TO FEEL GOOD ABOUT IT. TO UNWEAVE, GENTLY PULL
THE WEFT YARN OUT OF THE WARP, ONE ROW AT A TIME. WHEN YOU
HAVE UNWOVEN ENOUGH, START WEAVING AGAIN.

Unweaving can improve not only your weaving, but also your life! A woman named Penelope, a character in a very famous pair of poems about ancient Greece called *The Iliad* and *The Odyssey*, managed to keep a group of obnoxious men from ruining her life by spending her days weaving and her nights unweaving.

Penelope had been left alone to manage her kingdom for nearly 20 years because her husband, Odysseus, had gone off to fight in the Trojan War. The war took 10 years (its story is told in *The Iliad*) and Odysseus spent another 10 years trying to get home (the story of *The Odyssey*). When a group of ruffians moved into her castle insisting that she marry one of them (they thought that Odysseus must be dead after so much time), Penelope kept them away by telling them she couldn't remarry until she had woven a shroud (a special piece of cloth used to cover a dead body) for her father-in-law. To be sure she wouldn't finish, Penelope cleverly wove all day and then secretly unwove each night. After Penelope had been weaving and unweaving for about 4 years, Odysseus finally returned and chased the men away. After that, Penelope's weaving probably went faster and Odysseus, hopefully, kept his adventures closer to home.

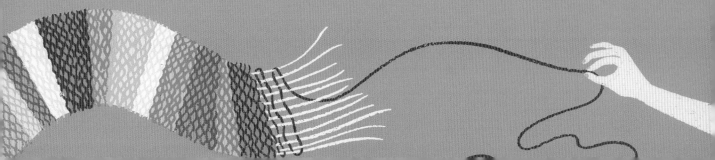

magic carpet graphs

*To make a pile carpet with a picture on it, you need to follow a pattern on a graph.
There are 3 graphed patterns at right for you to choose from. You can also make your own.
Each colored square on the graph represents one knot of a certain color. Every row of squares is
one row of weaving. Place the book next to you while you are weaving or photocopy the graphs in
color and tape the copy to a side bar of your loom, so that you can look at it while you weave.*

To use the graphed design, first notice how many squares there are. The designs for this project are 22 squares wide, so you will be making 22 knots across. Each knot is made on 2 warp threads, so 22 knots use up 44 warp threads. You have 52 warp threads, however 4 threads on each side are not knotted but are instead woven as protective edges. Your first knot, which will be the right or left edge square on the bottom row of your graph, will be made on the fifth and sixth warp threads in from one edge. Follow the colors shown on the graph or choose your own palette.

You will make 1 row of knots at a time. To keep track of the row you are on (so you don't get confused), you may want to cover the rows above the one you are working on with a piece of paper (use a paper clip to hold it in place).

When you finish each row of the graph, slide the paper up to reveal the next row.

making your own graph

To make your own graphed pattern for this warp, mark out an area on a piece of graph paper that is 22 squares wide and 28 squares tall (or photocopy the blank graph at right), then lightly draw your design (picture) onto the graph paper so that it fits inside your marked area. With a pencil, fill in squares to match your design. Sometimes it is hard to decide which square to choose if your lines don't match the squares, but this can be the fun part of designing. It might take several tries until your design looks the way that you want it to—some designers erase a lot! When your design pleases you, fill it in with colored pencils and choose yarn colors to match.

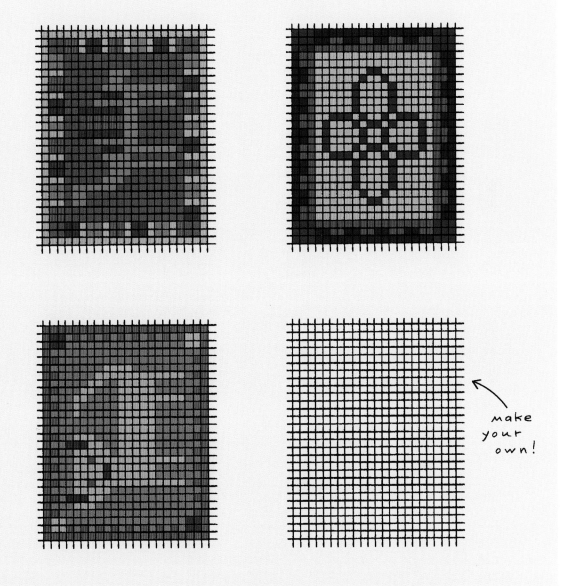

make
your
own!

Learning More

NOW THAT YOU ARE A WEAVER, YOU ARE PROBABLY NOTICING WOVEN THINGS ALL AROUND YOU AND THINKING, I COULD MAKE THAT! THE PROJECTS IN THIS BOOK WILL GET YOU STARTED AND KEEP YOU BUSY FOR AWHILE, BUT YOU'RE SURE TO WANT TO MEET OTHER WEAVERS AND LEARN ABOUT OTHER WAYS TO WEAVE.

Finding help

Below are some ideas of ways to find weavers in your area.

Ask at the local yarn or craft shop. There may be a local weaver happy to answer questions or become your advisor or mentor.

Look for a nearby weavers or fiber arts guild—groups of weavers often form organizations called guilds. These guilds usually have regular meetings where members talk about weaving, share their knowledge, and discuss the things that they have made. To find one, call the local chamber of commerce.

Contact the Handweavers Guild of America (1255 Buford Hwy, Suite 211, Suwanee, Georgia 30024; www.weavespindye.org; 678-730-0010). This wonderful organization has an informative website, puts out a quarterly magazine called *Shuttle, Spindle and Dyepot*, and also keeps track of smaller groups of weavers all over the country.

Attend a conference. HGA puts on a huge national conference called Convergence every other year, where there are workshops and seminars on every topic imaginable as well as the most unbelievable weaving-related shopping. Smaller regional weaving organizations put on their own conferences, often on the years when there is no Convergence—HGA will have information about those.

Weaving on other looms

One kind of loom that you might have seen and want to try is a treadle loom. These are particularly good looms for weaving large pieces of cloth or complicated patterns with more than two sheds (combinations of threads that are up and threads that are down). You can learn more about these kinds of looms from a local weaving store or from books, but here is an illustration to get you started.

kids embroidery
kids crochet
tapestry weaving

heddles
beater
warp
cloth
warp beam
shed
shuttle

Sources *for*
Supplies

Brown Sheep Company

(Navajo Wool Warp and Lamb's Pride Bulky Wool)

100662 County Road 16

Mitchell, NE 69357

(800) 826-9136

www.brownsheep.com

Earthues

(Natural dye extracts and mordants)

5129 Ballard Avenue NW

Seattle, WA 98107

(206) 789-1065

www.earthues.com

Harrisville Designs

(Highland Style Wool)

Center Village, P.O. Box 806

Harrisville, NH 03450

(800) 338-9415

www.harrisville.com

JCA, Inc.

(Paternayan Persian Yarn)

35 Scales Lane

Townsend, MA 01469

(508) 597-8794

Straw Into Gold

(Crystal Palace Cotton Chenille)

160 23rd Street

Richmond, CA 94804

(800) 666-7455

www.straw.com

Unicorn Books and Crafts Inc.

(12/12 Seine Twine and Klippen Asborya Wool)

1330 Ross Street

Petaluma, CA 94954

(707) 762-3362

www.unicornbooks.com

Recommended Reading

Stories and woven cloth seem to go together naturally. Some pieces of woven cloth, called tapestries, have stories woven into them as pictures. Other stories are made of written words rather than yarn but are about special pieces of cloth. The stories listed here are among my favorites.

Picture Books

The Goat in the Rug
Charles L. Blood
A goat and a Navajo weaver work together to spin, dye, and weave the goat's fleece into a rug.

A New Coat for Anna
Harriet Ziefert
Anna's mother trades with a spinner, a weaver, and a tailor, and Anna is warmed both by the coat and by her community.

The Legend of the Persian Carpet
Tomie dePaola
A weaver helps a king and, in the process, he and his fellow apprentices create a carpet.

Los Ojos Del Tejedor: The Eyes of the Weaver
Cristina Ortega
Christina learns Hispanic weaving and family traditions from her grandfather in northern New Mexico.

Master Weaver from Ghana
Gilbert Ahiagble and Louise Meyer
Traditional weavers of Kente cloth in Ghana, West Africa, pass the skill from father to son, weaving together both threads and a way of life.

Novels for Young (and not-so-young) Adults

Juniper
Monica Furlong
The process of becoming a wise woman includes learning to weave one's own magical cloak.

Lyddie
Katherine Paterson
A young girl goes to work in a cloth factory in Lowell, Massachusetts, determined to make enough money to reunite her family.

The Fellowship of the Ring
J. R. R. Tolkien
Galadriel and her maids in Lothlorian weave magical cloth that is made into protective cloaks for the 9 companions of The Fellowship.

The Lady and the Unicorn
Tracy Chevalier
The story of the creation and weaving of the series of world-famous tapestries by that name.

map doll templates

To use these templates to make the **Dancing Map Dolls** on page 16, photocopy and enlarge them to 165%.

girl

Acknowledgments

As it is always best to start at the beginning, I must mention that this book began as a twinkle in the eye of Melanie Falick, my visionary editor. I cannot thank her enough for her effort, ideas, talent, taste, and, not least, willingness to learn the difference between warp and weft.

Chris Hartlove took all of the beautiful photos and it was an absolute pleasure to work with him. Lena Corwin turned words and rough sketches into clear and charming illustrations, Beth Huseman helped make sense of my words, and Julie Hoffer and Jessi Rymill put it all together, a remarkable achievement.

For testing my instructions I heap praise upon the head of Bryn Ohlgren-Evans, who has been with me on this odyssey from beginning to end, and Talia Candler, both ever ready to tell me when my instructions were totally dumb. I also very much appreciate the work of Emily Alexander, Henry Edwards, Katie and Andrew Gammon, Hannah and Carolyn Knaack, Sebastian Mortimer, Nevada Sowle and Katherine Stegner, all of whom, along with their divine parents, provided important feedback.

Thanks always to the fabulous Hog Heaven Handspinners, the members of the Palouse Hills Weaver's Guild, and my talented friends in the weaving and spinning communities, for their ideas, interest, and support, and particularly to Helen Bobisud, first to read the entire manuscript, and Sara Lamb, who not only served as a technical editor but also, along with Archie Brennan, generously shared loom design ideas with weavers everywhere.

I am everlastingly grateful to my parents, Shiela and Steve Swett, for welcoming the photography crew to Vermont and so generously allowing us to take over every inch of their house, lives, and beautiful property, and also to the Vermont Alpaca Company, for allowing us to finish our photography on their land.

My heartfelt thanks go to Kristen Petliski (imaginative stylist), Robin Ohlgren-Evans (associate wife), Lyn Miller (one and only sister), and every one of our magnificent models: Sara Birenbaum, Sarah Hampton, Bryn Ohlgren-Evans, cousins Sophie and Charlie Janeway, my fabulous son Henry Edwards, Willow the dog, and the enthusiastic parents (and owner) thereof.

For life, the universe, his cooking, and everything, I thank my husband, Dan Edwards.

Index